FREE RANGE HUMANS

EXPOSING THE MATRIX CONTROL SYSTEM AND AWAKENING YOUR TRUE SELF

MATTHEW STEPHEN

Print ISBN: 9780994205339
Ebook ISBN: 9780994205346

To my family and friends, thank you for your love, support, and patience while I completed this book; I couldn't have finished it without you. Thank you to the amazing renegade truth seekers whose research and insights played a major role in the creation of this book and the direction it took. Thank you to my soul family who are scattered all across the planet right now. Some of you have already awakened and have remembered who you are and your mission here, whilst some of you are still waking up. I acknowledge the courageous and amazing work you are doing, wherever you are, and I hope this book is valuable to your mission. Finally, thank you to my beautiful wife Stephanie for always being there for me and for your endless support and patience in helping me to get this book finished. Particularly for constantly challenging me to make my writing more concise and compelling. I could not have done this without you.

FOREWORD

Be careful. We're surrounded by them. Individually they can be dealt with, but in herds they can be very dangerous. Don't make any sudden movements or speak too loudly. Keep your head down and shuffle along in whatever direction they're going. By blending in, they won't attack you.

Some call them zombies. I prefer a friendlier sounding term: *normal people.*

What does it *mean* to be normal? If we go by what society rewards and punishes, being normal means: don't question reality, don't think for yourself, obey authority, believe what the news tells you, trust the government, and ridicule those who question the official narrative. Like the walking dead, there's something creepy and unnatural about this programmed, mindless, hypnotized mode of existence. And yet, simply because it's so popular, it's come to define what "normal" is.

Are you a normal person? Not if you're reading this book. At some point in your life you must have started wondering, questioning, *suspecting*. You were compelled by a sense of *wanting to know*. While normal people prefer simply not knowing and staying asleep, you were curious and brave enough to start looking for answers. And that brings you to this book.

The available information out there is a vast and tricky minefield to navigate. Some books say little despite so many words. Some just rationalize pet theories that miss the mark. Some are sneaky sales pitches for expensive products or cult-like agendas. It takes a lot of time, energy, and discernment to cut through all that verbiage and get a clear perspective of what's going on. Fortunately, Matt has done exactly that.

This book will save you time and get you up to speed on the most critical challenges we face and how to tackle them. I say this sincerely as a veteran researcher myself. My process of awakening began early in life via a childhood haunted by paranormal phenomena. I was not a normal kid, but then my reality wasn't normal either. Since I was intensely curious by nature, the conflict between wanting to understand it all and being confronted with the unexplainable set me on a lifelong quest to figure it out. For the next three decades I read hundreds of books, networked with thousands of people, and gained years of experiential data to help connect the dots.

Along the way I met other researchers who were probing the deepest mysteries of our time. Like climbers of a mountain all converging upon the same peak, no matter where each started, we were all independently converging upon the same higher understanding of reality. Matt belongs to the few who didn't simply stop at the first convenient belief system he encountered. There are many ideological traps out there that offer permanent rest for the weary in the form of pat answers. It takes a good deal of self-honesty and intuition to go past them and keep ascending that mountain. And the higher you go, the broader your perspective.

Free Range Humans is colossal in its scope and hits the mark straight on. It's designed to help you attain freedom and happiness in the face of systematic oppression and control. See, mankind today is like a prisoner hypnotized into thinking he's free. To actually be free, he must first see the prison for what it is. Only then can instructions on breaking out make any sense. That's why a good portion of this work is dedicated to unraveling the illusion, exposing the forces who run this control system, and helping you recognize the covert manipulations present in your own life.

The author does this not to be alarmist, but to be *empowering*. By understanding the scope of the problem, the solutions make so much more sense. The key is recognizing that the forces seeking to keep us spiritually asleep and programmed aren't just the political, corporate, and religious powers of this world. Rather, it extends beyond the physical into the metaphysical domain. So the solutions must likewise include metaphysical considerations to have any chance of success.

The final part of *Free Range Humans* is therefore devoted to what we can do individually and as a society to transcend this Matrix-like control system and establish a more prosperous and positive future. It's not about marching in the streets, starting some new religion, or infiltrating government; these are external attempts at change that hack the branches instead of striking the roots. Without giving too much away, it's about discovering the hidden spiritual power within us and pivoting everything else upon that fulcrum.

This is not a normal book for normal people. It's a tool of awakening, a catalyst for empowerment. It's for brave, open minded, curious seekers who have begun suspecting that our world is *not* as it seems.

Thomas Minderle, author of montalk.net
Boca Raton, Florida

IMPORTANT DEFINITIONS

The following is a list of definitions that will be helpful to the reader throughout the book. Some of these definitions have been taken with permission from the website www.montalk.net.

Astral body: The astral body is a component of our being that mediates the thoughts of Spirit to the etheric body, and communicates the impressions of the physical body to the Spirit. The astral body is the seat of our feelings, desires, impressions, and passions. Its energies are active in our subconscious.

Astral plane: Also known as the "inner planes," is a nonphysical environment comprised of the energies of consciousness rather than configurations of matter. One can access it only through the mind, by retreating from the outer physical or etheric world and turning within. The dream world, the afterlife, and the astral plane are all closely related.

Avatar: A Soul and Spirit that have incarnated in physical form without suffering from the past life and spiritual amnesia that nearly all other beings experience. An Avatar being is fully self-realised, and in full service to their Divine mission, and they tend to be great teachers for humankind.

Cognitive dissonance (cognitive): meaning "*the mental action or process of acquiring knowledge and understanding through thought, experience, and the senses.*" Dissonance meaning "*a lack of harmony*" (Oxford English Dictionary, or, OED).

Therefore, cognitive dissonance describes a mental state that occurs when someone receives information that directly conflicts with their current belief systems, thus causing internal mental disharmony. The typical symptoms of this are emotions such as anger, frustration, indignation, and fear, often resulting in disbelief, shock, defensiveness, and rejection of the information that was received.

Density: Density is a measure of a being's level of conscious development; each density corresponds to a particular stage in the evolution of consciousness. For instance, lower densities have more rudimentary lifeforms operating by simpler laws. Higher density beings are more sophisticated in mind, body, and soul.

> *First Density (1D)* is the lowest, corresponding to subatomic particles, atoms, molecules, chemicals, and minerals, where conscious development is rudimentary and limited to simple awareness.
>
> *Second Density (2D)* are plant and animal life, where consciousness first experiences will, passion, drive, pain, or pleasure.
>
> *Third Density (3D)* includes beings like ourselves, who possess the seed of self-awareness and freewill. Consciousness makes the choice between helping others or exploiting them.

These three densities are fully physical and subject to the limits of three-dimensional space and linear time. They inhabit the same physical realm. Also, the densities blend into each other, and within each density there is a gradient from the lowest to the highest evolved types of beings. This is clearly seen in 2nd Density where the lowest forms such as sponges or bacteria are not on the same level as the highest such as primates.

> *Fourth Density (4D)* includes beings that straddle the boundary between spacetime and the higher ethereal realms. For them, physicality is plastic and responsive to thought. They exist behind the dimensional curtain and can project into our reality at will. Some are positive, others are negative. Both 4D beings and their environments are part physical, part ethereal. The spiritual goal of 4D existence is to fully live out their choice of spiritual polarity (negative or positive). Telepathy and supernatural abilities come easily.

Fifth Density (5D) is a completely ethereal level of existence, functioning as a stopover zone for departed souls and a native realm for beings who have evolved to that level. Native 5D beings seem focused on accumulating wisdom and total perfection of their individuality.

Sixth Density (6D) is where individual entities have finished their personal evolution and group together to evolve as a soul group. They exist as energy beings in a realm completely outside spacetime.

Seventh Density(7D) is "unity with the Creator" and the total dissolution of individual existence, though not through annihilation of consciousness but achievement of infinite consciousness that permeates all life and all existence.

Density can also refer to the native realm inhabited by beings of a particular level of evolution. For instance, to "be in Fourth Density" means to be in a realm natively inhabited by Fourth Density beings. Since such beings live in a quasi-physical state between physical and ethereal, Fourth Density as an environment or realm is likewise quasi-physical. It is the superset to our rigidly physical realm, the room to our fishbowl. In Fourth Density, spacetime is more fluid, flexible, and responsive to consciousness. It is an etherically potent environment.

Disillusionment: Means to have one's false illusions of the world dissolved. It is a process of discovering and realising that something is not as it originally appeared to be, and is often accompanied by feelings of shock, disappointment, resentment, and anger. In this book, "disillusionment" is used to describe a stage of awakening that the seeker must go through in order to discover and awaken their true self.

Ego personality: An artificial intelligence in the soul and brain that helps a being operate more successfully within a particular environment. The environment programs the ego into the soul through the intellect. Beings like plants and lower animals who lack intellect also lack egos.

When the ego is an instrument of Spirit, it provides an individuality and personality through which Spirit can accomplish its purpose in the physical realm. In that case the ego takes a large part of its programming from Spirit, as it's partially operating in a spiritual context and thus a spiritual internal environment.

When the ego breaks away from Spirit, or if Spirit is absent, then the ego becomes solely a product of the physical environment and picks up all the traits of physical living—survival and competition, primarily. Then it starts exploiting others for the sake of self-gain. Lying, deception, manipulation, delusion—these are the properties of ego if left unchecked by Spirit. Ego removed from Spirit is the foundation of the STS (service to self) pathway.

But it is as much an error to annihilate the ego, because then one becomes ineffectual in this world, unable to carry out the mission of Spirit with discernment, vigour, togetherness, and focus. Rather, the ego must be conquered and reprogrammed, refined and sharpened, to act in accordance with the impulse of Spirit.

Esoteric: This term refers to traditional schools of thought that focus on the development of one's inner world, and the awakening of the true self. It also relates to a study of the Universe and understanding Man's place within it. In her book 'The Reality of Being', Jeanne de Salzmann succinctly writes; *"Esoteric knowledge is the science of man's relation with God and the universe"*. I have been particularly inspired by the esoteric works of George Gurdjieff, Rudolf Steiner, Pyotr Ouspenskii, Boris Mouravieff, Joseph Campbell, Herbert Shelton, Carl Jung, and Paul Brunton.

In modern times I have been most influenced by the esoteric works of Bernhard Guenther, Paul Levy, David Icke, and Tom (Minderle) Montalk.

Etheric energy: Lifeforce energy that also serves as the "source code" of physical reality. It is a subtle energy scaffolding that mirrors, permeates, and surrounds physical matter and lifeforms. Changes to the etheric create corresponding changes in the physical.

Hyper-dimensional: A higher dimensional density to our third density dimension.

Law of the Jungle: The law of the jungle is the realm in which most humans exist. It is a realm based on survival, competition, ego, and service to self. It is the natural realm on Earth, and it causes man to prey on his fellow man on every level imaginable, and is a large reason why man-made laws are required in order to limit the amount people can exploit each other. Those who become spiritualised, however, are able to transcend the law of the jungle and can instead operate within the realms of higher spiritual laws. These laws are based on service to the Great Spirit and service to others, and they are characterised by traits such as nobility, wisdom, love, and a pureness of heart.

Loosh: Another term for lifeforce/emotional/spiritual energy. It is a term coined by Robert Monroe in his astral voyages where, upon interacting with nonphysical entities, he learned that this energy was called "loosh" and that mankind was being farmed for their loosh.

Matrix Control System (MCS): A matrix is defined by OED as *"the cultural, social, or political environment in which something develops."* Therefore, when I refer to the MCS, I am referring to the cultural, social, or political environment in which we humans develop. More specifically, the MCS is a deliberately engineered container that is designed to be a system of human control. It includes everything one might consider oppressive in Third Density Earth life, such as governmental, legal, military, political, and educational systems, mainstream media, Hollywood, pharmaceutical, and religions, etc., to the influence of negative forces in the Fourth Density realms and higher.

NHF's: This is an abbreviation for Negative Hostile Forces. These are beings of a highly negative, predatory, and evil nature who feed off the negative emotional loosh that humans are manipulated to produce.

Objective: A state of perception whereby one understands and perceives themselves and the world exactly as they are, not influenced by subjective blind spots and wishful thinking.

Occult: This is related to spiritual forces, either negative or positive, that are hidden from view.

Orwellian: A term derived from George Orwell's famous 1949 novel titled *1984*. It is generally used to describe anything related to his depiction of humanity's future being controlled and ruled by a dystopian totalitarian state. Referring to something as "Orwellian" also insinuates that it is deceptive and means the opposite to what it says. For example, if an Orwellian world government says that it intends to implement measures to increase the safety of society, it really means that it intends to implement measures to increase its control over society.

Realm: The sphere of your influence and experience, your own reality bubble. Those who inhabit a common realm share common experiences and have some commonality in their Frequency Resonance Vibration. Two entities residing in completely different realms have little in common and are not mutually aware of each other. Realms regarded as "higher" can observe the activities of "lower" realms but not vice versa, as the lower realms are subsets of higher ones. Realm, dimension, and density are interchangeable terms in certain cases.

Renegade: A person who is willing to stand up and resist any form of tyranny, whether it arises from a person, organisation, or ideology.

Soul: A nonphysical energy field belonging to living beings, comprised of etheric and astral components. It allows Spirit to interface with the physical body. The soul can exist apart from the physical body, and even apart from Spirit. Just by itself, the soul is equivalent to a thoughtform.

Spirit (also referred to as the "true self", "higher self", and "true I"): Spirit is the core of individualized consciousness within oneself, which survives death and rebirth and can continue growing in its complexity and intensity through numerous physical forms. It is the God-spark within that eventually achieves congruency and unity with God. Spirit is most developed in the Higher Self, and the two are essentially synonymous. Spirit is also the true source of freewill, empathy, and wisdom.

Spiritual Embodiment: The full integration of Spirit within the physical body so that it can manifest its will through the flesh and into Earth density.

Subjective: A state of perception of the world and oneself that is distorted by personal bias, inner beliefs, conditioning, and wishful thinking.

HERE WE ARE, A DISTANT STAR, STUCK IN A GALAXY SO VERY FAR.

LIKE A TANGLED VINE, CUT FROM THE DIVINE, WE
CAN ONLY RETURN IF OUR HEARTS ALIGN.

LIKE A CANCEROUS CELL, OUR EGOS SWELL, ONLY
TIME WILL TELL IF WE CAN RESCUE OURSELVES.

OUT OF THE HEAD, AND INTO THE HEART, IS THE ONLY
THING THAT WILL TEAR THIS SYSTEM APART.

COURAGE TO FIGHT WITH ALL OUR MIGHT, BEFORE
DARKNESS DESCENDS, AN ETERNAL NIGHT.

TABLE OF CONTENTS

INTRODUCTION

There is something very wrong with the world; you have sensed this for a long time. Why are we so divided? Why is there so much war, violence, and hate? Why aren't people accepting and nice to each other? Why are we afraid to tell each other how we really feel?

These questions have lingered in your mind since you were a kid. You wish you could communicate them to people and explore them more deeply, but no one else around you seems to think in the same way. Every time you try to go deeper with people, they just shut down. What is wrong with them? Everyone is walking around like zombies, living their lives and moving about as if all of this madness is normal. This world you have found yourself in is… strange.

Not knowing what else to do, you attempt to join them and try to mould yourself to the "normal" values of your society. What are these values? Well, to get to work following the life plan, of course! You know, that plan that we all must follow? Go to school, go to university, build a career, make money, pay your bills and taxes, buy a house, get married, have a family, get a dog, pay off your loan, go on vacations, and plan for retirement. These are the things that create happiness and are what life is all about, right? So, you pursue them just like everyone else, but... the happiness never comes. Every time you reach a milestone of your life plan, you still feel... empty and anxious. Sure, you may feel good for a while, but it doesn't last. That inner peace and fulfilment that you feel is possible, that you feel you deserve, just never comes. So, you keep striving and striving, grinding and grinding, believing that a greater effort and focus will finally bring you lasting peace and happiness, but it doesn't. Even worse, not only does the peace and happiness never come, but the price you pay for your relentless striving is great. You develop chronic stress, anxiety, deteriorating health, broken relationships, addictions, neurotic habits, control issues, and then there is that... thing. That presence that is always there, a lingering darkness that surrounds you like a fog. It makes you afraid to be alone, afraid to reveal your true thoughts and feelings to the world, afraid to be rejected, and afraid that you aren't loveable. This is the inner reality for many people around the world.

The path commonly taken from here is that we keep striving and pushing ourselves to the point where we self-destruct. This may manifest physically in the form of an illness or disease, emotionally in the form of an anxiety attack and burnout, or psychologically in the form of a depression or mental breakdown. Or, possibly all of the above. We may also find ourselves sabotaging everything we have achieved in our lives.

This self-destruction and the suffering it creates catapults people down different paths. For some it will trigger them into a pit of despair, hopelessness, and victimhood from which they may never recover. Often these people will choose to numb themselves and disassociate completely, checking out of their body and of life through the various addictive habits that are available. For others, it will instead trigger them to awaken. To snap out of their hypnotised mechanical slumber, like a sleepwalker suddenly regaining consciousness, which allows their true self to begin to emerge.

This awakening causes us to eventually reject the "normal" cookie-cutter plan of life laid out for us from birth by society, and to instead pursue what the true self came here to achieve. In this regard, no one path is the same, and there is no "right or wrong", just choices, consequences, and lessons, all of which contribute to our personal awakening and spiritual evolution. This is why expecting that the same life plan will work for everyone is insanity. The challenge is that the true self is hidden under layer upon layer of societal and cultural programming, conditioning, and traumas; therefore, discovering and reconnecting with it requires peeling away everything that blocks our access to it. To achieve this demands courage, determination, sincerity, and knowledge of the various forces, both physical and non-physical that seek to keep us programmed, hypnotised, and enslaved. We are not without help, though, for we are guided by our intuition, which is our direct connection to the true self. As well, if we are open to receiving them and carry ourselves with sincerity, many helpful synchronicities will be placed on our path. This can manifest as the right teacher, event, or piece of knowledge appearing in the perfect place at the perfect time. If we are receptive to their messages, each synchronicity will open up a new layer of understanding and awareness, both of ourselves and of the world.

Higher awareness, however, also brings forth new challenges and responsibilities, for as we awaken and spiritually evolve, we begin attracting the attention and attacks of the Negative Hostile Forces (NHF's). NHF's are comprised of higher density predatory beings, occult (hidden) parasitic entities, and their psychopathic human puppets. The primary goal of the NHF's is to keep us in a hypnotised mechanical slumber with the rest of the herd, so that we can be more easily controlled and utilised to serve their agenda. In order to achieve this, they have engineered what researchers call the Matrix Control System (MCS).

The MCS is designed not only to control humanity and keep us imprisoned on our own planet, but also to allow the NHF's to farm us for our most precious substance—our lifeforce energy. I mean this quite literally, for the reason that the NHF's are so interested in us is because we are a valuable source of food to them. We are like the "free range" animals that we farm, who in truth are not really free, but whom we allow to roam "free" in their paddocks because it benefits us to do so. If we intended for them to be truly free, then we would remove the fences that keep them confined, but we do not permit this for they serve a purpose. They are our source of food, just as we are a source of food for the NHF's. For this reason, we allow them to roam within a specially assigned space, give them food to eat, water to drink, and friends to socialise with, so that they maintain their health and produce a high-quality product when it is time for them to be harvested.

Just as an animal within its fenced-off captivity believes itself to be free and therefore senses no danger, so too do we humans believe we are free, but this freedom is just as illusory. We are given the *perception of freedom* only because it serves a purpose to our masters. Our allotted "paddocks" are certainly bigger than the ones we provide for the animals that we farm; these paddocks are what we call countries. Don't believe me that we live in a giant captivity? Try leaving your "country" without permission from your masters. Try doing nearly anything, in fact, without permission from your masters. Because the illusion of our freedom must be upheld, the NHF's begrudgingly allow us to roam around within our paddocks, or possibly to visit another paddock from time to time. However, this is only allowed within the parametres of their strict rules, regulations, and intense Big Brother surveillance, which they cleverly convince us exist for "our own safety". In truth, just as there are free-range animals, so too are we *free-range humans.*

Awakening to the horror of our situation can be extremely confronting, but it is something we must face or else we will never obtain our freedom. A true awakening demands that all of our false illusions must come crumbling down, and all darkness must be revealed, no matter how shocking or disturbing it is. That is the purpose of this book, to support you on your journey of awakening by helping to dissolve any remaining illusions.

The key to awakening is knowledge, and that is why for the MCS, deception and suppression of knowledge is the name of the game. The knowledge found in this book is exactly what the MCS and its architects do not want you to obtain, for it holds the keys to helping you transition from a free-range human, to a truly free and awakened being.

Many books of this nature speak with strange sounding esoteric lingo or in abstract terms that allude to the truth, but often in an ambiguous and difficult to decipher language. This book attempts to do the opposite, and instead communicates in clear, direct, and concise terms.

However, just because the information within is clear and concise does not mean it will be easy to digest. Quite the opposite, in fact, as the topics it tackles are confronting and directly opposing to the perceptions and beliefs programmed into us by the MCS. Despite this, I am confident that if you take this journey with me, you will find this book immensely liberating and empowering.

The question you need to ask yourself is if you are truly ready to take this journey? For, if you do not wish to have your familiar and comfortable perceptions of the world deeply challenged, and possibly even shattered into pieces, then I would suggest thinking twice before reading on. As there are many people who say they want to awaken, but as spiritual teacher Adyashanti explains, "*...most people who say they want awakening don't actually 'want to awaken'. They want their version of awakening. What they actually want is to be really happy in their dream state.*"

CONTENT AND FLOW

This book is broken up into three sections. It is written in such a way as to expose you gradually to the information it contains, so that the information can be better digested and absorbed.

Section 1: I describe the awakening that is occurring around the planet, including what we are awakening from, and the various stages of awakening.

Section 2: I describe the Matrix Control System, a system set up by higher negative predatory beings who seek to keep humanity imprisoned, using their human puppets to push forward their agenda of a New World Order. I will also outline this New World Order and its endgame agenda in detail.

Section 3: Using the knowledge obtained in the first two sections, I then describe how we can transcend the Matrix Control System prison on both a personal and collective level.

Please buckle in, for I am going to take you on an interesting ride, and hope you enjoy the journey.

SECTION I

THE AWAKENING

CHAPTER I

THE MATRIX CONTROL SYSTEM CULT

1: HOW CULTS ENSNARE US

"The victim of mind-manipulation does not know that he is a victim. To him the walls of his prison are invisible, and he believes himself to be free. That he is not free is apparent only to other people. His servitude is strictly objective."

~Aldous Huxley, *Brave New World*

A difficult issue to contend with when presenting people with the alternative and potentially controversial information found within this book is the cognitive dissonance that can arise. This is an uncomfortable mental state that occurs when we are confronted with information that directly challenges and conflicts with our currently held perceptions and beliefs. Cognitive dissonance commonly triggers reactions such as shock, disbelief, fear, and anger, and causes us to reflexively reject what we have been presented without any consideration or further research. People are also often resistant to this sort of information, because they consider themselves to be intellectual and aware beings. Therefore, to be told that they have been deceived their entire lives and are living in a control system without them being aware of it is an affront to everything they have been taught to believe. For it directly challenges their deeply ingrained belief that they are 'free beings', as well as challenging their sense of pride that accompanies this belief.

To understand how we can all be so easily ensnared and deceived by the Matrix Control System (MCS), regardless of having an advanced intellect, requires us to understand that the MCS is a powerful cult.

The OED defines a cult as *"A system of religious veneration and devotion directed towards a particular figure or object."*[1] However, to understand this definition better, it is helpful to understand the definitions of 'religious', 'religion', and 'veneration'.

> Religious: *"Relating to or believing in a religion."*
>
> Religion: *"The belief in and worship of a superhuman controlling power, especially a personal God or gods."*
>
> Veneration: *"Great respect; reverence."*

With these extra definitions in mind, we could more plainly and simply define a cult as *"A system of great respect, reverence, belief, and worship directed toward a superhuman controlling power."*

We can now begin to realise that we have all been indoctrinated into a cult from birth.

We have been programmed to revere, believe in, and be blindly obedient to the "superhuman controlling powers" that we know as government and monarchy.

Many cults have appeared throughout human history, giving us ample evidence and data to study how they work and why they have such a strong influence over the human mind, even the minds of the supposedly smartest and wisest of humans.[2] What we have learned is that cults lure people in by preying on their vulnerabilities and wounds. They understand these weak points within their victims, and they exploit them by offering what appear to be alluring solutions and remedies for their suffering. *"Worship us, worship our "God", be utterly devoted to us in every way, and we will save you and heal you of all your pains"*, the cult will say, either openly or subliminally to its target. Many people uncritically accept and believe what is being promised to them by the cult because when we are wounded, we are vulnerable to external suggestions, especially if those suggestions have been presented with conviction and authority. On top of this, a cult makes its members feel special and like they belong, and this gives them a sense of acceptance and purpose, things that they have been longing for their entire lives. A cult also commonly triggers a saviour complex in its victim, fuelling them with a distorted but burning passion to go out into the world and recruit as many other members into the cult as possible. This person genuinely believes that they are helping others "see the light". Thus, using each cult member as its instrument and puppet, the cult grows its sphere of strength and influence victim by victim. A cult member at this stage of the process cannot be reasoned with, for their cult programming and highly inflated self-importance blinds them from being able to see their position clearly and objectively. As a result, what is obvious to others becomes invisible to the victim.

Once a cult has lured its vulnerable target in, it then capitalises by relentlessly indoctrinating them into the values and beliefs of the cult. This is achieved by pummelling their minds with endless propaganda, which they will deceive them into believing is enlightened esoteric and sacred knowledge. A typical part of this propaganda within most cults is to convince their members to anticipate the arrival of a "saviour" or a "God", or to believe that one of the leaders within the cult is the saviour himself. Most cults also nearly always declare that the end of the world and destruction of humanity is imminent, except of course for those who are the most obedient to the cult and its saviour, for they will instead be "saved".

The cult then ensures that this programming is not reversed by any outsiders who are yet to be brainwashed by warning each member against *"those who will try to deviate them from their path and corrupt their beliefs"*. The cult will tell them that these people haven't yet "seen the light" and therefore can't be trusted. This then makes the victim highly suspicious of and even aggressive toward anyone from the outside who attempts to challenge their cult programming. This in turn makes it very difficult for others to help them see the situation they are in, which of course is by design.

The programming effect on the human mind by a cult is a very interesting phenomenon. It is as if the cult places firewalls in the minds of its victims, causing them to reject any outside information that conflicts with their programmed beliefs. This is similar in concept to how countries like China place firewalls on their nation's Internet, blocking citizens from being able to view certain websites. Once these firewalls have been implanted, they are very difficult to remove.

On top of this, often the victim becomes emotionally dependent on his or her new masters, and this creates a distorted but very deep bond that is extremely difficult and painful to break. This is particularly the case if the victim has been previously traumatised and therefore has a low self-esteem. This distorted bond is a form of Stockholm Syndrome, a phenomenon whereby a victim becomes so accustomed to and dependent on their captivity that they do not wish to leave, and even begin to worship and defend their captors.

Another key characteristic of a cult is that it inevitably becomes possessive and paranoid about controlling every element of its members' lives. This is not always perceptible at first, for the cult does not want to scare them away by being too overbearing too soon. But once it has lured them in, it will gradually increase the level of commitment that it demands from each member. It will begin monitoring and tracking them obsessively, demanding to know everything they are doing and thinking, every single moment of the day. It will begin enforcing strict rules and will seek to censor and punish anyone who is disobedient. It will force each member to wear a special uniform, to recite certain prayers or mantras, to eat certain foods, to talk in a certain way, to adopt a certain sexual preference, and even to stop seeing close family and friends. These are just a few of the endless things that a cult wants to control. As a result of all these factors, a cult dehumanises its members and turns them into unthinking mechanical robots, utterly obedient to anything the cult demands of them.

2: THE GLOBAL CULT

It is only by studying and understanding how cults work that we begin to realise and come to terms with the reality that we have all been ensnared by a giant global cult.

However, the MCS cult, or what I will often refer to as simply the Cult, is one of the most dangerous and powerful cults that has ever existed. For it does not even give us a choice as to whether we want to be a part of it or not, as it traps us from birth and programs us before we have even had the opportunity to think for ourselves. By the time we can think for ourselves, we have already been so well indoctrinated into the Cult that we never even think to question our life within it, or seek to escape from it. Of course, many of us do sense that something is very wrong with the world, but the Cult is designed to make us feel like we are the crazy and weird ones for thinking that way. We are like animals born on a farm, who, despite sensing deep within that something is wrong with their environment, cannot comprehend their captivity simply because they have never known anything else.

Just like how animals on a farm are conditioned to perceive their human masters as being all powerful, we are also conditioned to believe that the Cult's institutions of government and monarchy have a God-like status that endows them with immense power over human life. Such as the power to impose endless rules and regulations onto every part of our lives, to leech away our hard work through ever-increasing taxes, and to punish and lock us in a cage if we do not obey. This conditioning runs so deep that even the thought of disobeying government, or any associated "authority", brings up fear and anxiety in most people. We are taught that government is there to ensure "peace and order" in society, and that society would fall into an uncontrollable state of anarchy and violence without it, but this is just another one of the web of lies embedded into our Cult programming. The truth is that government is just a tool for the Cult to do to us what every other cult in history has done, which is to monitor, track, censor, and control every single thing we are doing every single second of the day. This is so that the true architects of the Cult, those that operate from within the shadows of the MCS, can prey on and exploit the human race solely for their benefit.

This information, however, cannot be grasped or understood through the lens of our Cult programming, as we must first peel back the layers of lies and deceptions one by one. This can be a painful and messy process as the Cult traumatises us from birth, making us feel unsafe and insecure, and creating deep wounds that it can then exploit throughout our lives. In fact, it has turned indoctrinating and exploiting the human race into a fine art. Just like every other cult in history, the Cult we are in is also trying to convince us that the end of the world is imminent. It is also trying to convince us that we can all be "saved" by merging our biological body's with artificial intelligence and robotics through what they call "transhumanism".

3: BREAKING THE SPELL

Once the Cult's spell begins to lift, all illusions that previously distorted our perception of reality start to shatter, and we begin to see the world *very* differently. What was once "normal" suddenly begins to appear very alien and foreign. We begin to realise that the world is absolutely nothing like it seems, and that everything within the Cult is based upon a lie. This will seem like an extreme and exaggerated statement to those still influenced by the Cult's spell, but once the spell breaks, and its programming is removed, this truth becomes very apparent.

To make things even more challenging, there are many smaller cults within the Cult that can also trap us. Whether these be based on religious, political, cultural, corporate, or even dietary ideologies, it does not matter. If we have found ourselves within *any* group that demands that we worship and blindly follow its beliefs and commandments without questioning its authority, we are in a cult.

How then do we break free from the Cult?

History has demonstrated that if the members of a cult are sufficiently indoctrinated, they will blindly follow its commandments without question, even if those commandments are clearly irrational, dangerous, and deadly. As well, in these circumstances, no outside help will be effective in awakening them to their situation, at least until the victim is subjected to a series of experiences powerful enough to shock them into a state of disillusionment. This disillusionment then frees the victim temporarily from their spell, and they begin to see their situation clearly for the first time.

Generally, the only thing powerful enough to trigger a state of disillusionment like this is when the cult leader or leaders become so intoxicated by their power that they begin consistently abusing it. Thus, they begin to slowly reveal their true predatory nature and subsequently heap a great deal of suffering upon the cult members. Due to the fact that their true nature is so contrary to the "virtuous and holy saviour" images they originally portrayed themselves with, the victim will receive a major shock. It is this shock that will hopefully jolt and awaken them out of their blind and submissive state of hypnosis.

What this means is that in order for people around the world to break free from the spell of the global Cult, each person must experience a level of suffering powerful enough to trigger within them a similar state of shock and disillusionment. This is already occurring on a massive scale, as millions of people around the world are already becoming disillusioned with their world leaders and governments, who—intoxicated with power—are beginning to reveal their true predatory natures more and more. However, many are still under the spell of the Cult, and whilst they remain this way, we find ourselves in a very dangerous position. This is because cults of the past have shown us time and time again that when blind faith and obedience is given to predatory leaders and their systems of control, the end result is never good.

CHAPTER 2

AWAKENING TO THE ILLUSION

1: SPIRITUAL AWAKENING

To effectively free ourselves from the Cult requires not just awakening from our state of mechanical hypnosis, but also requires a *spiritual awakening*. This is because it is only through gaining the higher awareness of our true self, or what I will often refer to as *Spirit*, can we effectively perceive the world from a more objective state of awareness. This then allows us to see beyond our deeply embedded Cult programming.

A crucial part of experiencing a spiritual awakening is first coming to terms with the reality that we are much more than just flesh and bones. We are instead eternal spiritual beings having a temporary and fleeting human experience, inhabiting an intelligent biological technology that we call the human body. The human body performs a function similar to a receiver and transmitter antenna, whereby it receives the energies and awareness of Spirit, and then transmits these energies into Third Density Earth life. On top of this, the body also receives the energetic information of Third Density Earth life through its senses, and decodes this into what we can touch, hear, feel, smell, and taste. This information is then transmitted to Spirit, allowing it to experience what we call "physical reality" in a way that it could never experience without the body. How this occurs more specifically, as well as a deeper look into the nature of our reality, is something we will explore in Chapter 12.

Unfortunately, for most people, their Spirit remains asleep and suppressed beneath all of their Cult programming, and they instead only experience the world through the extremely limited and mechanical human ego. Our mission and challenge therefore is to re-awaken Spirit, which allows the ego to become spiritualised and to be placed in service to Spirit, which then allows Spirit to pursue the mission it came here to fulfil.

Despite inhabiting a unique body that gives us a sense of independence and identity, our Spirit emanates from and is always connected to a single unified field of intelligent energy. This field is what is commonly referred to as "God", the "Creator", the "Divine", the "Great Spirit", "Brahman", "Allah", "Krishna" or in quantum physics as the "Quantum field". There has been much religious distortion and dogma around these terms over the millennia, which has turned many people away from spirituality. This too was a strategic ploy by the Cult, whereby it hijacked human spirituality and converted it into a system of dogmatic control (organised religion) designed to vector people away from true and authentic spiritual connection. Many people have been negatively affected by this and subsequently have lost faith in a higher power, but we should not let this manipulation take away from the reality of who and what we truly are.

2: THE INTERCONNECTED WEB OF LIFE

Whilst inhabiting the human body and being subjected to its limited range of sensory perceptions, we adopt the illusion that we have left this unified field of pure energy, which I will often refer to as "Great Spirit", and that we now live in a world of separation. This, however, couldn't be further from the truth, as everything within the Universe is unified. This is why it is called the *uni*-verse, meaning "one-tune" or "one-rhythm", indicating that the Universe is a dance of energies all playing to the same tune and rhythm, unified and conducted by the Great Spirit. This unification of all things is evident even in our physical world, despite things certainly appearing to be divided to the naked eye. For example, we see a tree and a bird and we believe them to be independent from each other, and yet we find that they are unified by the same atmospheric field of oxygen, nitrogen, and carbon dioxide on which they both depend. Therefore, no line of division could be accurately drawn between them as the atmosphere literally lives merged within their cells and DNA.

This means that to create a boundary around them, you would have to include the entire Earth's atmosphere within it. Similarly, if we were to include Earth's atmosphere within our boundary around the tree and the bird, then we must also include the Sun. For the Earth's atmosphere cannot exist without the radiation of the Sun, and no distinct divide could ever be found between the two. If we were to include the Sun within our boundary, then we must also include the entire solar system which the Sun's radiation reaches. We must then also include the entire galaxy and Universe. No divisions can ever be found in the Universe as it is a singular organism, and everything is interrelated in some form or another. The Cult has deliberately kept this understanding from us, because when we think that we are living in a world of separation, we feel lonely, insecure, powerless, and afraid. On the other hand, when we realise that not only are we eternal, but we are always connected with each other and with the entire Universe, then we realise how pointless it is to be afraid. Without this fear, the Cult loses its power over us.

3: THE PARADOXICAL WORLD OF QUANTUM PHYSICS

On top of everything being interrelated, nothing in our reality is solid, either. Even the most solid seeming objects such as rocks and trees are made up of atoms; these atoms are made up of particles that exist in a state of pure vibrating (nonphysical) energy. Even more amazing is that they also consist of 99.999% empty space![3] This means that the apparent solidity of the things we see in the world, including ourselves, is nothing more than an illusion. The appearance of solidity is created within our brain, similar to a very realistic virtual reality simulation. This also points to the fact that the world is not even "out there" as it seems, but rather only exists within our brains and minds as we decode it through the body. Before we decode it, it exists as energy. Again, this is something the Cult does not want us to understand, for when we realise the illusory nature of the physical world, and that we are only here for just a fleeting experience to learn and grow, we realise the illusory nature of death. When we lose our fear of death, the Cult again loses a major source of power over us.

In the 1999 blockbuster movie *The Matrix*, Morpheus refers to the illusory nature of the world when he says to Neo, *"What is real? How do you define 'real'? If you're talking about what you can feel, what you can smell, taste and see, then 'real' is simply electrical signals interpreted by your brain."*

In his 2019 book titled *Quantum Revelation*, author Paul Levy also explains that, "*Physics tells us that matter is composed of more than 99.9999999 percent empty space. In Eddington's words, 'Matter is mostly ghostly empty space.' How do we wrap our mind around this? The new physics has discovered that matter is a pulsation of energy temporarily emerging out of a deeper substratum of boundless, unmanifest potential that creates the illusion of solid objects in three-dimensional space. This illusion is fabricated within our brain and nervous system in such a way that a physical world appears to be really there outside of us, when in fact its real basis is a neurologically generated standing wave holographic pattern that is witnessed by consciousness in such a way as to trick us into seeing it as a solid, external world of physical objects. Our physical world can be likened to clouds in the sky. Seen from the ground, clouds look like substantial objects, but if we 'enter' the clouds while flying in an airplane, we discover that there is no hard-and-fast boundary around them. They simply dissolve into a fine mist. Quantum physics reveals that the same is true for our world, which appears substantial, and yet at bottom is just an endless series of unpredictable fluctuations whose ultimate existence is transitory and insubstantial.*"

Quantum physics has also revealed through famous experiments like the double slit experiment that human consciousness and physical matter cannot be separated, and that the act of human observation alone changes the way matter behaves. In the double slit experiment, which has now been repeated numerous times with the same results, photon particles changed their behaviour when they were being observed. It's as if they were conscious and understood they were being watched and didn't want to be caught out acting in weird ways. They acted as pure energy patterns when not being observed, but acted like particles when they were observed. This points to the fact that the physical world (which is comprised of photons) only acts physical when we observe it, and when we are not observing it simply exists as energy. Levy explains that, "*So not only does the photon know whether both slits are open or not, it also knows whether or not we are watching it, and adjusts its behavior accordingly. It is as if the photon knows beforehand that we are lying in wait ready to observe it and, as a result of this, chooses to maintain its particle persona. Appearing self-conscious, the photon doesn't seem to want to be seen in its quantum weirdness, as if not wanting to be caught in the act of going both ways at once. If the detector at the slit is turned off, we then have no knowledge of the route the photon has taken, its secret is safe, and it resumes its mysterious wavelike behavior and the interference pattern comes back. The photon not only knows which slit is open or closed, but seemingly possesses information about the whole experimental setup, including the observer, which in principle suggests that it knows the quantum state of the entire universe.*

"This suggests that the quantum world is truly sentient, as well as holistic; each of its parts are in touch with the whole. There is no clearer example of the interaction of the observer with the observed than the double-slit experiment. Consciousness interfered in the experiment in such a way so as to have a direct effect at the quantum level. It is important to understand that Wheeler's idea of a participatory universe was not based on wild theoretical speculation, but on the most rigorously tested scientific experiments imaginable. Quantum theory is so counterintuitive that he could never have dreamt it—even in his wildest dreams—without the constant guidance provided by experiments. The double slit experiment was the very first experiment in which consciousness literally entered the physics lab in a way that was both impossible to ignore and demanding to be accounted for; there were countless other types of more elaborate experiments to follow. The double slit experiment helped to reveal the dual, seemingly schizophrenic nature of the quantum world. It was the experiment that first showed that how light manifested—as a wave or a particle—depended upon how it was observed. This is the prototypical experiment that revealed how consciousness not only was an inextricable part of the universe, but actually affected the very universe of which it was aware through the act of awareness itself. 'Consciousness,' as Bohr reminds us, 'is inseparably connected with life.'"

To put this all in the simplest language, what this means is that our human awareness alone—the act of simply observing—changes the way reality reacts. This suggests that we are co-participating in the creation of the reality we see each day, which means we are co-participating in the creation of the Universe. This means that we are much more powerful than we have ever been led to believe.

One difficult thing to come to terms with is the evidence that things do appear to exist when we are not observing. For example, we can leave a forest unobserved for years and come back and it has clearly grown and changed in physical ways despite not having an observer there to decode it. Levy addresses this conundrum: "*The question naturally arises—what constitutes an observer? This is one of the central and most burning philosophical questions in quantum physics. In addition to humans, what about a cat, a mouse, a cockroach, an amoeba, or a piece of mica? How does their observation differ from human observership? Are there observers that help shape the universe that do not have physical bodies? The spiritual traditions of the world are replete with accounts of just such kinds of observers, after all. If so, is there a cooperative collaboration between these disembodied observers and the more fully embodied ones in which all the parties involved are cocreating how reality unfolds? Where does consciousness first enter in the elaborate hierarchy of terrestrial life? Where does the capacity to collapse a wave function derive from? Does it come from the presence of consciousness or from some other condition? It's as if observership and its ability to translate unmanifest possibilities into definite actualities is a pervasive feature which is widely distributed throughout the web of life. In any one observation, the entire universe is in some way implicated and participating. From this perspective all life-forms are dreaming together, collectively collapsing the universal wave function of this universe to manifest the way it is moment by moment."*

In an essay published in the scientific journal *Nature*, Professor Richard C. Henry also addresses this issue: *"The 1925 discovery of quantum mechanics solved the problem of the Universe's nature. Bright physicists were again led to believe the unbelievable—this time, that the Universe is mental. According to Sir James Jeans: 'the stream of knowledge is heading towards a non-mechanical reality; the Universe begins to look more like a great thought than like a great machine. Mind no longer appears to be an accidental intruder into the realm of matter... we ought to rather hail it as the creator and governor of the realm of matter.'"*[4]

The architects of the Cult understand who and how powerful we are, and they are desperately afraid of us realising this power. Their primary goals are to keep us spiritually asleep, in a state of perpetual fear and stress, ignorant of the nature of this reality, and believing that we live in a meaningless mechanical Universe where everything is divided. The Cult maintains these states amongst the masses by engulfing us in a culture of ignorance and disinformation, largely helped by the institutions of mainstream science, media, and education. The basic message we receive regarding who we are is that we are just random bunches of cells clumped together by chance, and that our consciousness is just a random lucky side effect of the complex human brain. This means that once our physical body dies, so too does our consciousness end, forever. This disempowering way of understanding who we are leads many people to feel hopeless, meaningless, powerless, and vulnerable, which is exactly what the Cult wants.

There is evidence everywhere of our nonphysical and spiritual nature as human beings, but this of course is not the sort of "proof" that will satisfy those indoctrinated into the Cult. Most have been too deeply conditioned to believe that unless something can be seen and touched, then it can't be proven. When one studies the science of quantum physics, however, it becomes apparent that this incredible field of study is helping us to bridge the gap between science and spirituality.

4: OUR SPIRITUAL ORIGINS

On top of the science of quantum physics, humanity has also had many other channels of information reaching us from the higher densities, providing compelling evidence that we are eternal spiritual beings at our essence. There have been numerous examples of enlightened spiritual avatar masters who have incarnated on Earth throughout our ancient and recent history to share their spiritual wisdom. Providing us with clear road maps as to how we can once again reclaim our connection to the world of Spirit.

There have also been numerous accounts of what are called NDE's (near death experiences) whereby people have been pronounced clinically dead and then brought back to life. During the period of being dead, they experienced their Spirit crossing a threshold into other realms of pure energy. They recognised these realms as their true spiritual home and were able to come back to report on what they saw. Another similar example is scientist Jill Bolte Taylor who did not die but had a stroke which changed the way her brain decoded reality. This gave her an incredible experience of being attuned to a nonphysical energetic world that she recognized as the true spiritual home of our existence. She shares her story on a now famous Ted talk titled "My stroke of Insight".

Many people have claimed to experience the higher spiritual densities of consciousness through the use of psychedelic plant medicines such as Ayahuasca, Psilocybin mushrooms, Peyote, San Pedro cactus, and other psychedelic drugs such as LSD, DMT, ketamine, marijuana, and MDMA. Of course, these experiences are argued by some to be simply the result of chemical changes in the brain. Yet the overlapping specific details of people's experiences from all around the world when under the influence of these psychedelics are too remarkably similar to just brush aside without further contemplation and investigation. Many see and experience the exact same things on psychedelics, pointing to the possibility that these chemicals unlock gateways to higher densities. It is also no accident that all of the drugs that expand spiritual awareness are the ones that are condemned and have been made strictly illegal in nearly every country around the world by the Cult. Whereas drugs that limit spiritual awareness (such as alcohol and pharmaceuticals) are not only made legal but are largely encouraged and normalised. This makes sense, for the goal of the Cult is spiritual suppression at all costs, and therefore they must take away all tools that could provide us with helpful spiritual insights. This is not to say that psychedelic drugs are necessary to expand spiritual awareness; they are simply tools that can be used if the seeker is so drawn to them. It has been shown by many cultures around the world that we can establish a more permanent and less artificial connection with the spiritual densities through drug-free techniques such as meditation, dancing, rhythmic breathing, chanting, prayer, and shadow work.

There are also many psychic healers and clairvoyants who are born with more sensitive psychic centres and abilities. As a result, they can see and perceive the spiritual realms and observe their inhabitants such as angelic or demonic entities with much greater clarity than the average person.

As well, just about every continent on the planet contains indigenous cultures that have held strong beliefs about the spiritual realms for many thousands of years. One such ancient indigenous tribe from the Malaysian jungle named the Sng'Oi, who were documented in the book *Original Wisdom*, believes that this physical world is a shadow world and when we go to sleep at night, we enter the true world via our dreams. Viewing this belief through the indoctrinated mind of the Cult, it can easily be laughed off as primitive nonsense and myth. However, as one spiritually awakens, it becomes clear that many so called "primitive" indigenous cultures have encoded great truths about the Universe within their myths, stories, art, and architecture.

CHAPTER 3

SPIRIT, BODY, AND EGO PERSONALITY

Essentially, man is made up of three core components, that being *Spirit, body*, and *ego personality*. There is also a soul component, which I view as the interface between Spirit and body. To keep things simple, and because there are conflicting ideas on the differences between the Spirit and the soul, I will focus on the three core components just mentioned. The highest functioning of these is of course Spirit, which is the eternal and immortal part of ourselves. It remains beyond the death of the physical body and also exists in a realm of complete oneness; beyond the dualities we experience here on Earth. The next component, the body, is what anchors our higher density Spirit into our current lower Third Density earthly realm, allowing Spirit to temporarily experience life as a human. The body comes equipped with its own instinctive intelligence, which is highly attuned to ensuring survival within the harsh and volatile Earth conditions. This intelligence focuses largely on self-preservation, regeneration, and procreation, ensuring that primal requirements such as food, water, sex, rest, avoidance of injury and predators, touch, and comfort are adequately obtained. The body communicates these needs to us through sensations, drives, impulses, and emotions. It can also communicate messages from Spirit to the ego through what we call intuition.

The third component, the ego personality, is an illusory creation of the mind that arises from one's beliefs, ideas, experiences, education, and conditioning. This includes one's name, nationality, religious beliefs, titles (such as doctor, lawyer, sportsmen, parent, etc.), likes and dislikes, habits, and so on. It is illusory because nothing within the ego personality actually exists in tangible form, it is instead comprised of labels that we have given ourselves and then identified with as being real. Despite being illusory, the ego personality is still an important component of our being as it brings individuality to each person and allows for uniqueness of expression as Spirit and body move around in Third Density. However, the ego personality can become dangerous and destructive when it is severed from the voice of Spirit, and when we falsely identify with it as being the true self.

1: IN SERVICE TO SPIRIT

Under ideal circumstances, there is complete harmony between these three core components of man. As the body and ego personality surrender their will to the will of Spirit, both honouring and trusting its supreme wisdom and higher guidance. In this scenario, both of these components function as tools for Spirit to utilise in order to express its will on Earth. As a result, they both become spiritualised and undergo a profound transformation.

For most, however, this is far from the case. As a result of the spiritually oppressive conditions created by the Cult, most people are severed from the voice of Spirit, and are solely identified with the body and the ego personality. Therefore, without the governing will of Spirit, the body intelligence and ego personality are forced to take control and make the executive decisions as each person moves around in their lives. In this very common scenario, Spirit only has the power to passively observe the activities of life from the background.

The main problem with this situation is that the body's intelligence is not an ideal master as it is focused solely on primal matters, with the main one being survival. If our lives become dictated by survival only, then we operate within the law of the jungle, which is the mentality of "eat or be eaten". The law of the jungle is where most people operate, and whilst strict man-made laws have attempted to minimise the violence and destruction caused by those operating under this law, man still preys upon man on every level imaginable. On top of this, the primal drives of the body that drive executive decisions can become hijacked and distorted through things such as chemically laden substances, overstimulation, and trauma. For example, if a child is raised on chemically altered and sugar-laden processed foods, then their body will develop a perverted and unnatural craving for these types of food in the future. Another example is someone who watches an excessive amount of porn, which distorts their natural and healthy impulses to have sex into extreme fetishes. Or, if a person has experienced a trauma, or a series of traumas that remain unhealed, then these can cause the body to become incredibly tense and in a state of stress (fight/flight) even when it is in a safe environment. In these circumstances, the body's instinctive commands begin leading one into a state of poor health, addictions, and irrational fear/paranoia, and thus cannot be fully trusted.

The ego personality is an even less ideal master, for without the higher guidance of Spirit, it is simply a by-product of its environmental conditioning and education. It will live a life and operate exactly in the way it was programmed to, and yet it will never admit to its ignorance for it is also engulfed with self-pride and arrogance. It believes that its intellect makes it a "superior" being. The ego personality is also heavily influenced by the primal drives of the body, particularly the drives of self-preservation, and seeking sex and sensory pleasure. This causes the ego personality to also operate within the law of the jungle, and to lie, cheat, manipulate, and exploit its fellow man in order to advance its own agendas. It also causes it to seek artificial pleasures such as drugs, stimulants, and indulging in excessive consumption of food. There is nothing necessarily wrong with operating within the law of the jungle, as this is the nature of third density life on Earth, and is the nature of the human body that Spirit inhabits. The law of the jungle simply means that we must do whatever is necessary in order to survive and advance ahead of all other lifeforms. For animals living in the wild, this is the natural way of living, and is the highest level of development they are capable of. We humans, however, have the potential alone to operate within the laws of the higher spiritual realms instead. This completely transforms the basis on which our life is oriented, and typically means our life becomes about service to others, and service to Spirit, rather than service to self. Living within the laws of higher spiritual realms can only be achieved by awakening Spirit, and allowing the body and ego personality to submit to its higher guidance.

2: THE REAL "I"

What occurs as a result of the body and ego personality taking control over one's being is that there is no continuous "I", and therefore the "I's" that we identify with are false, inconsistent, and contradictory to each other. One day we say, *"I' want this," "I' will do that,"* and *"I' feel like this,"* but then the next day we say the same things and yet express very different wants and desires. We believe that these differing wants and desires all represent the same "I" just changing its mind. In reality, they represent many different independent "I's", which is why they are often so illogical and contradictory. If these independent "I's" were to have any chance of working together in harmony toward the same goals, then they need a higher governing intelligence to bind them together. Without this governing intelligence they all pull one in various directions, and the inevitable result is conflict and chaos. In his trilogy series titled *Gnosis*, Boris Mouravieff likens this scenario as similar to allowing every citizen one hour each to completely control the country in which they live, making all authoritative decisions. One could imagine that the results would be grand chaos, conflict, fear, and confusion, just as it is in the lives of many humans. The human being contains only one supreme governing "I" that can bring unity and harmony to all of the other "I's", and that is the "I" of the eternal Spirit.

When/if one's Spirit awakens and begins to take control over the various "I's", it first has the grand job in front of it of healing the damage caused by these conflicting "I's" being allowed to run rampant for so many years. This is along with healing the traumas and negative programming installed by the Cult. The only way this healing can occur is through providing total and complete love, patience, and nurturing toward ourselves, just like we would provide for a wounded animal. Unfortunately, many instead treat themselves with disdain, criticism, and self-judgment, as well as placing major pressures on themselves to keep ploughing forward at a frenetic pace without ever slowing down.

CHAPTER 4

CULT INDOCTRINATION AND NEGATIVE PROGRAMMING

In order for Spirit to bring healing, unity, and harmony to the various "I's" of the body and the ego personality, it is important to understand exactly how and why our wounds and disfunctions came about. This next section is dedicated to investigating and revealing the ways in which the Cult indoctrinates and conditions us from birth, and subsequently instils much trauma and negative programming.

Please keep in mind that the things I mention here are just overviews; volumes of books have been written on many of these individual topics alone. I will cite a number of researchers and resources throughout this book so that the reader can pursue further study, or alternatively many resources can be found at www.seedsofawareness.com.au/resources/.

At the beginning of life, it is necessary for the healthy development of a newborn human to be raised in a household and within a family system that is unified, loving, stable, and largely free from stress. Infants also need a great amount of physical and emotional affection and attention from their parents, in particular the mother. For many, this is far from the case. A significant portion of people around the world are born into fragmented families that lack these qualities, and some are unfortunately born into verbally, physically, and sexually abusive families. These experiences can obviously create lifelong traumas.

Children are naturally pure, creative, embodied, loving, and open beings. They want to explore, learn, create, dance, play, and their imagination and belief in what they can achieve know no limits. These qualities are slowly and surely conditioned out of most children by the Cult as they grow up and enter puberty and adulthood. Many adults in a child's life play a big role in this by unconsciously passing down their own negative Cult programming onto them. This generally occurs insidiously over time, and unfortunately the child is far too young to discern what is happening. It can even arise from seemingly innocuous situations such as a child asking if he or she can grow up to be a famous actor and the parent/adult declaring with authority and disapproval that this is a silly dream, and that he or she needs to be realistic and strive for a "normal" career. Or by the parent/adult consistently commanding their child to "stop being silly", "stop playing around", "grow up and behave", "stop being naughty", "you could never do that", "that's a stupid idea", "act your age", etc., whenever the child displays his or her naturally curious and playful nature.

This insidious and often subtle style of programming may also occur when, for example, a child may be curious about spirituality, or about fairies, angels, and demons, and the adult replies indifferently, dismissively, or disapprovingly, by saying, *"Oh, that stuff's just make-believe nonsense"*. For sensitive young children who are looking for approval and validation from the adults in their lives, instances like these can be traumatic and cause them to eventually stop expressing and exploring their curiosities. As a result, a child's spiritual development can become significantly stunted and his or her self-esteem will be damaged. Or a child may be raised in a family that never talks about or expresses emotions and feelings, causing the child to bottle up his or her own emotions and feelings. Or they may never discuss topics such as death or sexuality, so the child forms the belief that these are "taboo" topics that are forbidden to speak about. This suppression can cause the child to feel shame or think that something is wrong with him or her whenever the perfectly natural desire to know more about those topics arises.

Another insidious method of Cult programming is when adults impose onto their child what they believe a "successful" human life should look like. For example, they may firmly believe that a successful life requires a "good education", a well-paying job, getting married and having a family, and placing savings aside for retirement in order to retire with security. There is nothing wrong with these values and they may work well for some children as they grow up. Other children, however, may not feel like this is the plan that they want to follow and may deeply desire to do other things that are more suited to their unique personalities and inner Spirit. Unfortunately, instead of being encouraged to follow their own path, they might receive immense pressure from their parents and the people around them to follow the more conventional path. This can cause them to carry around guilt and shame if they do not please them and live up to expectations. The parents and adults may have the sincerest intentions for their children, and firmly believe that they are teaching the children how to live a successful and secure life. What they don't realise is that what they are in fact doing is imposing their Cult programming down onto them, ensuring that they stay within the boundaries and guidelines of the Cult.

These are just some examples of how negative programming can occur in early life within the Cult, but it can also manifest in countless other ways. These are also some of the more subtle and insidious ways that children can be negatively programmed and wounded, as some are outright mentally and physically abused. The subtle negative programming, however, can be much harder to detect because it is not explicitly abusive, so children have no way of realising the programming and trauma they have received. They just assume that the way they have been conditioned to see the world, and the way they feel about themselves, is simply "normal".

The most important thing to understand is that children, especially up to the age of 7, are incredibly sensitive, suggestible, programmable, and crave validation and security from the authority figures in their lives. Therefore, whatever the main adults and authorities in their lives do or say on a daily basis, either negative or positive, will have deep impact on them.[5]

1: INSTITUTIONAL INDOCTRINATION

On top of being programmed by unwitting loyal members of the Cult throughout childhood, those being our family and close friends, the Cult has also set up powerful institutions to ensure that the indoctrination is deeply and firmly embedded.

OED defines an institution as *"An organisation founded for a religious, educational, professional, or social purpose."* Essentially, what it says here is that an institution operates as an organised container. A container that ensures that everything within it flows in the same direction and that nothing spills out over the edges. This means that an institution can also be used for the goal of indoctrinating and programming the people within it to submit to its will. This is exactly why the Cult has built itself upon institutions, because that allows it to keep all of its Cult members within the same container and to ensure they are all heading in the same direction.

The following is a brief look into these institutions and the impact that they have on our minds and bodies, and the damage they cause that must be healed once our true self awakens. Before I go on, I wish to add that I am not attempting to take anything away from the amazing work certain individuals do within these institutions. Some of these institutions, such as the education system, are showing signs of positive evolvement. However, these changes have only come about because of passionate and heart-centred individuals working extremely hard to make them happen, and have nothing to do with any truly benevolent actions from the Cult.

INSTITUTION 1 - EDUCATION:

A: MODERN DAY SCHOOLING

This is one of the most important institutions for Cult indoctrination, and the term "indoctrination" should really replace "education" as its correct title. The modern-day schooling system, whilst having some obvious positive elements such as teaching one how to read, write, learn arithmetic, and socialise, and admittedly is becoming more progressive in some areas, largely indoctrinates dangerous beliefs into the minds of children. Its main purpose is to create subservient, dumbed down, and submissive Cult members who do as they are told and are programmed not to question their masters. As a result, if one has been through twelve or more years of schooling, then once they awaken Spirit, they will discover that their "education" has created a significant amount of negative conditioning that must be undone. What makes this process harder is the fact that we are sent to school in the most formative years of our lives, ensuring that our indoctrination runs very deep. This does not mean it cannot be reversed; it just means that it will take a great deal of effort and discomfort.

John Taylor Gatto was a teacher for thirty years in New York City, and was named New York City Teacher of the Year in 1989, 1990, and 1991, and was also named New York State Teacher of the Year in 1991. After his career ended, he became a passionate and vocal critic of public education and subsequently authored a series of books that outlined his critiques. One of his most well-known books was titled *Dumbing us Down: The Hidden*

Curriculum of Compulsory Education. In this book, he declared that overall, school taught and conditioned seven key lessons into students. This was even if the teachers themselves were unaware that these underhanded lessons were being taught. Or to put this in other and more direct language, he discovered that school enforced seven major Cult principles that would ensure that the newly forming young Cult members would become unquestioning and obedient Cult adherents.

They are:

1. CONFUSION

Gatto explains that Nature works in natural sequences. When we learn to walk and talk, for instance, there are a series of sequences we learn over a number of months and years that follow each other in logical order. This gives us an internal sense of coherence and continuity, which helps us to understand what we are learning and why we are learning it. Everything else in Nature also follows this logical sequential pattern, from the way the sun rises and sets, to the way a tree grows, to the different seasons in a year.

The way school is taught goes directly against this sequential and logical flow, and heavily confuses the mind of a young child. Children are taught one thing in a classroom, and then just as they are grasping it a bell rings and they must instantly move to another classroom. Once there they must shift their attention straightaway to an entirely different subject. A child is thus not given a proper chance to develop any sort of internal harmony and coherence, and this can lead to inner frustration, anxiety, panic, and an inability to focus on a subject for any meaningful length of time. A child suffering from these symptoms will often be told that they have Attention Deficit Disorder (ADD) and may even be placed on drugs for it. Or they may be told that they have "learning difficulties". This feedback can damage the child's self-esteem as they begin believing that something is wrong with them.

2. CLASS POSITION

In many schools, children are placed in certain classes based on their judged intelligence, which is often based on standardized tests that do not take into account a child's unique strengths and gifts. Children are also mostly forced to be grouped with children their age, even if their level of development is not equal to others of their age. This is true whether they've been told that they are dumb, smart, average, poor, or wealthy. They are conditioned to simply put their head down, do as they're told, and obediently accept their position. This also conditions into children the idea of division and judging others purely based on their class positions. It also affects how children judge themselves; for example, children in the "smart" classes may develop an inflated ego and arrogance, and children in the less smart classes may develop a low self-esteem.

Gatto explains that, *"My job is to make them like it, being locked in together with children who bear numbers like their own. Or at the least to endure it like good sports. If I do my job well, the kids can't even imagine themselves somewhere else, because I've shown them how to envy and fear the better classes and how to have contempt for the dumb classes. Under this efficient discipline the class mostly polices itself into good marching order. That's the real lesson of any rigged competition like school. You come to know your place."*

3. INDIFFERENCE (LACK OF INTEREST)

In school, children are forced to learn many things that they are not passionate or excited about, and things that are mundane and mind-numbing and difficult to pay attention to. If they do not comply, then they are scolded and threatened with punishment and are often publicly shamed in front of the other students. To win approval and avoid trouble, children must force themselves to pay attention to a mind-numbing and anxiety-inducing subject, and then as soon as the bell rings, they must instantly switch off, move to another room, and then instantly switch on their full attention again toward another mind-numbing and anxiety-inducing subject. This teaches children how to feign interest whilst switching off their mind and dissociating in order to not go insane, something that conditions them to cope with mind-numbing and anxiety-inducing jobs they might perform later on as adults within the Cult. It also conditions them to become disembodied by having to suppress the natural urges in their bodies that beckon them to run around outside, explore, and play with other children. Suppressing these urges and disconnecting from the body also blocks their connection to their inner intuition, which is their connection to Spirit. As a result, they become much more programmable and mechanical and their spiritual development is stunted.

4. EMOTIONAL DEPENDENCY

As children, we desperately seek emotional approval and to be accepted by our tribe. School conditions us to believe that these rewards are given only when we display a certain set of behaviours. This forces us to suppress our uniqueness and individuality in order to conform to a cookie-cutter system to avoid being banished by the tribe. Banishment from the tribe is something that triggers deep and ancient primal fears.

This ensures that children become emotionally dependent on the Cult that they are being indoctrinated into, and in particular on the approval of the authorities within the Cult. This is an insidious but highly effective method of behaviour control.

Gatto explains that, *"By stars and red checks, smiles and frowns, prizes, honors and disgraces, I teach kids to surrender their will to the predestined chain of command. Rights may be granted or withheld by any authority without appeal, because rights do not exist inside a school—not even the right of free speech, as the Supreme Court has ruled—unless school authorities say they do. As a schoolteacher, I intervene in many personal decisions, issuing a pass for those I deem legitimate, or initiating a disciplinary confrontation for behavior that threatens my control. Individuality is constantly trying to assert itself among children and teenagers, so my judgments come thick and fast. Individuality is a contradiction of class theory, a curse to all systems of classification.*

"Here are some common ways it shows up: children sneak away for a private moment in the toilet on the pretext of moving their bowels, or they steal a private instant in the hallway on the grounds they need water. I know they don't, but I allow them to deceive me because this conditions them to depend on my favors. Sometimes free will appears right in front of me in children angry, depressed or happy about things outside my ken; rights in such matters cannot be recognized by schoolteachers, only privileges that can be withdrawn, hostages to good behavior."

5. INTELLECTUAL DEPENDENCY

In school we are taught what to think, when to think, how to think, and we are told how intelligent we are by the exact number or percentage we receive when we perform graded tests that were created by the authorities. This teaches us that our intelligence is determined by and dependent upon an external authority. If this authority tells us we are smart, dumb, or average, we must obey and not question this judgment. This imposes within the minds of children certain limitations and boundaries that they believe they cannot cross.

As well as emotional and intellectual dependency, I would also argue that school teaches physical dependency. It does this by teaching very little to nothing regarding skills necessary for physical independence and survival. Things such as how to build shelter, how to grow food and develop permaculture gardens, how to hunt or forage for food, how to find clean water, how to lead others and cope in times of emergency, how to start a fire without matches, how to know which plants are medicinal and which are poisonous, how to treat wounds, how to spot and stay clear of predators, and so on. As a result of this lack of serious training in these crucial areas of human life, most of humanity is now completely and utterly dependent on the Cult for their survival, and therefore completely and utterly dependent on those who control the Cult.

6. PROVISIONAL SELF-ESTEEM

Just in the same way that our emotional and intellectual confidence is dependent on the judgment of authorities, so too is our overall self-esteem. At the end of every term, a child is given a percentage grade, and a meeting between the school and her parents is set up to provide feedback as to how well she is achieving. If the child is doing well by the school's standards, and is being a well behaved and obedient student, then she is endowed with encouragement, rewards, and her self-esteem is nourished. On the other hand, if she is not an obedient student, she will receive negative feedback, bad grades, and possibly threats of punishment, including being held back a grade. As a result, her self-esteem plummets, as does her confidence and motivation. This programs the child to believe that her self-esteem is dependent upon her obedience to the school, and later on in life, dependent upon her obedience to the Cult.

7. ONE CAN'T HIDE

Teachers are at all times watching and monitoring their students' every move, and some schools may even have surveillance cameras. This prepares the child for a life of constant Big Brother public surveillance within the Cult and ensures that they are already accustomed to a world where privacy does not exist. Children are also encouraged to tell on each other if another kid is doing something outside of the rules that the authorities have set. This is how Cult members are conditioned to keep each other in line and obedient to the Cult, and is also one reason why Cult members attack other members when they attempt to break free.

Gatto explains that, *"I teach children they are always watched, that each is under constant surveillance by myself and my colleagues. There are no private spaces for children, there is no private time. Class change lasts three hundred seconds to keep promiscuous fraternization at low levels. Students are encouraged to tattle on each other or even to tattle on their own parents."*

B: OBEDIENCE TO AUTHORITY

"Evil people rely on the acquiescence of naïve good people to allow them to continue with their evil."

~Stuart Aken

Essentially, in school, children are programmed to believe in and be blindly obedient to authority, and as Gatto describes in his books, school was not designed this way by accident. He succinctly explains that, *"Schools teach exactly what they are intended to teach and they do it well: how to be a good Egyptian and remain in your place in the pyramid."*

In order to achieve this, school first programs into the minds of the students that the world consists of only two groups of people: rulers and followers. In school, teachers are the rulers and the students are the obedient followers, and the school is the "all-powerful" institution that teachers unquestionably represent. This institution dictates the rules that students must be obedient to, and the things that they must learn. In school, students must do exactly what they are told, and they are rarely if ever allowed to question anything or speak out of line; however, teachers are given the power by the schooling institution to do exactly those things. Teachers can speak whenever they want, can create strict rules for the students to follow, and can punish students whenever they are supposedly "out of line". In the past, these punishments were even given in the form of physical violence.

What this conditions into the mind of young students is that not only does the world consist of rulers to whom they must be obedient to, but that these rulers have been endowed with powers of control that they do not and can never possess. As a result, by the time they finish their schooling, they are already conditioned to accept the mechanisms of the Cult, which contain the same hierarchical setup. This includes a society that consists of rulers who we know as politicians and royalty, and the "all-powerful" institutions that they represent known as government or monarchy, which endow them with the power to rule over the masses.

Because of the supposed power that the government institution provides them, politicians are allowed to implement laws that completely abuse human rights, leach vast volumes of money away from the masses, plunder the environment, and send millions to their deaths in wars, along with many other atrocities, and get away with it. In fact, governments, monarchies, politicians, and royalty, with all of their rules and regulations, now control modern human life down to the smallest degree. This situation is allowed to occur because the average human is so deeply programmed to believe in and be blindly obedient toward authority during their time in school.

Let's revisit our definition of a cult: *"A system of great respect, reverence, belief, and worship toward a superhuman controlling power."*

Based on this definition, it is very clear that school was deliberately designed to create programmed members of the Cult. For it perfectly conditions us to have *great respect, reverence, belief, and worship toward the superhuman controlling power* known as government, as well as those "authorities" who represent government. For those who do not like governments and authorities and their imposing rules, which is a very large majority, it still programs them to fear them and believe in their authority, and thus remain obedient to them.

This obedience to authority programming is so deeply engrained in most people that to challenge it in anyway can trigger cognitive dissonance. Most people even experience physical symptoms of distress and anxiety whenever a perceived authority figure is near. To have blind obedience to authority, however, is a very dangerous mentality because it causes individuals and mass groups of people to give their power away to those who are very eager to exploit it. It also causes us to follow immoral and unethical, or even downright psychopathic commands, because we have been programmed to be obedient to these authoritarian commands rather than listen to our own inner moral compass. This is how and why governments are estimated to be responsible for the deaths of over 200 million people in the twentieth century alone[6], because good people were programmed to take psychopathic orders without question from those in authority.[7]

C: DIVISION

School also conditions children to believe that the world is made up of many different groups who are all divided from each other. To achieve this, school teaches them to identify themselves with some of these groups and their values. These groups can be larger groups such as a nation, state, or a political group, or smaller groups such as a sporting team, their own school, and even smaller groups with their school. The number of groups are endless, and once we identify with one or more of them, it allows the Cult to divide and rule us much more easily. To establish a child's identification with a specific group, school will teach them to love and worship certain emblems, symbols, and anthems within that group. The national flag, anthem, and emblem are great examples of this, but every other group that the child is coaxed into will also have its own unique emblems, symbols, and anthems to be identified with. School also forces children to wear "uniforms", ensuring that they remain grouped together in "one-formation". These uniforms will also have specific school logos attached to them, which is yet another symbol and emblem for them to identify with.

D: CREATING THE NEXT GENERATION OF WORKERS

Another key purpose for school is to create the next generation of adult workers for the Cult ruling class to utilise and exploit as they wish. This is achieved by providing children, particularly those in public schools, with dumbed-down educations that equip them with only enough knowledge to become employees, rather than having the knowledge to become innovative and creative entrepreneurs.

In *Dumbing Us Down*, John Taylor Gatto says, *"I've noticed a fascinating phenomenon in my thirty years of teaching: schools and schooling are increasingly irrelevant to the great enterprises of the planet. No one believes anymore that scientists are trained in science classes or politicians in civics classes or poets in English classes. The truth is that schools don't really teach anything except how to obey orders. This is a great mystery to me because thousands of humane, caring people work in schools as teachers and aides and administrators, but the abstract logic of the institution overwhelms their individual contributions. Although teachers do care and do work very, very hard, the institution is psychopathic—it has no conscience. It rings a bell and the young man in the middle of writing a poem must close his notebook and move to a different cell where he must memorize that humans and monkeys derive from a common ancestor."*

E: THE WORLD IS COMPETITIVE

School conditions students to view the world from a competition-based perspective, and to believe that in order to succeed one must compete with and beat their fellow students. This is achieved by creating many tests whose scores depend on the students performing better than their fellow students. Certain schools will of course promote a team-oriented culture and will encourage students to work together, but overall the government curriculum that they are forced to teach will be based on competition between students.

F: FRAGMENTING THE BODY'S INTELLIGENCE

School conditions the student to view the world through only a fragmented part of the body's intelligence. The body-centres most directly connected with Spirit are the intelligences found in the gut and the heart. These types of intelligences do not communicate through analytical and abstract thinking like the brain in the head does, but through feelings, sensations, emotions, and intuitive knowing. These centres are how Spirit speaks to us, and yet school conditions us to experience the world mostly through the head-brain alone. Living in the head, we become numb and desensitised to the vibrant intelligence of the body as a whole, as well as disconnected from Spirit. School teaches us that the body is nothing more than a mechanical lump of flesh that evolved solely to carry around and keep alive the all-powerful brain in the head. This is in contrast to the truth, which is that the entire body is alive with intelligence and intuitive/instinctive wisdom.[8]

Our attachment to the head-brain and disconnect from the body's intelligence only becomes more severe and rigid the further we move through the schooling system. By the end of university/college, it is common for a person to have a highly developed intellectual knowledge of the world, and yet a significantly underdeveloped emotional and intuitive (spiritual) intelligence. In the esoteric tradition of Hermeticism, the knowledge one acquires about the world through learned education is known as "dead" knowledge, with "living" knowledge being that which is learned through personal experience, self-discovery, and a connection with Spirit. Knowledge gained intellectually rather than experientially is considered "dead" because once learned, it calcifies into a rigid belief system and an unmovable framework of the world. By filling our minds with dead knowledge, the Cult can program us with rigid beliefs that reinforce our obedience to the Cult. Living knowledge, on the other hand, is always evolving and expanding, and therefore is flexible, adaptive, dynamic, and cannot be programmed or moulded in any way.

Our fragmented intelligence goes even deeper, for the head-brain is also well known to have two separate hemispheres that view the world differently. The left side is responsible for analytical/logical thought, language, science, mathematics, numbers, writing, and reasoning. The right side is responsible for holistic/spiritual thought, creativity, imagination, music/art, insight, and intuition. School teaches us in a style that encourages us to mostly use the left hemisphere of the brain instead of both the left and right together. It achieves this by awarding higher marks and more accolades to students who perform well in left-brain dominant subjects, such as science and mathematics. This is in contrast to students who perform well in right-brain dominant subjects, such as art, drama, and music, which are generally marked lower and aren't considered as important within the government curriculum. By doing this, school insidiously teaches the students that right-brain dominant subjects will not lead them to any great achievements in the world. Therefore, in order to receive the validation and "success" they are seeking, many students shut down their creative passions and place most of their energies into the pursuit of left-brain dominant subjects. This then ensures students are well prepared to enter a very head-centric and left-brain dominant Cult.

INSTITUTION 2 - RELIGION:

As spiritual beings, it was natural that schools of spiritual thought were developed within certain human circles, and this eventually spawned religion. Some religions teach great truths and understandings of the Universe, including man's place within it. Many of these truths are embedded into religious texts and art, and are hidden in plain sight within stories, myths, symbols, and allegories, and can only be properly deciphered by those who have undergone esoteric development. For this reason, many stories and allegories within religious texts and art are taken literally and are therefore greatly misunderstood. On top of this, over the centuries, certain groups have created churches that allowed them to institutionalise religion and manipulate sacred esoteric knowledge in order to generate vast power and control over the masses. These churches have been converted into powerful cults that program distorted dogmatic "spiritual" principles into the minds of their worshippers. Often, they use fear as a tool of control by conditioning their members to fear their "God", and to feel like they are always being watched and judged. This "God" is often personified into an image of a stern older man with a beard, demonstrating the churches arrogant anthropocentric view of the Universe. They also teach that the priests of the church are the only ones who have the authority to communicate with their God and to translate his message. This ensures that not only are the members of the church cult often in fear of displeasing their God, but they are completely obedient to and in worship of the priests who supposedly represent God.[9]

Institutionalised religion via the church has operated as a way for the Cult to trap people who are seeking esoteric knowledge and inner spiritual development within smaller cults. This allows them to be programmed with distorted spiritual truths and ideologies, which then vectors them away from a true awakening, and manipulates them into worshipping dark satanic forces. Some countries have even utilised the power of their institutionalised religion to create a hive-like colony where literally everyone in the entire country must conform to the same ideologies. This is justified because it is done in the "name of God". In fact, many horrifying atrocities have been carried out in the "name of God".

Finally, and most disturbingly, certain churches are now well known to attract people who pose as enlightened priests, but are in fact predators who relish the chance to abuse the power that their position provides them. This is why there are so many reports of sexual abuse and paedophilia amongst some churches.

INSTITUTION 3 - MATERIALIST SCIENCE:

Materialist science believes that the fundamental building blocks of Nature are physical, rather than energetic, which means that everything can be explained by the cause and effect of physical phenomena. It also teaches that Nature is not alive and intelligent, but rather is mechanical and operates purely as a result of mechanical laws. This means that everything we see in the Universe has been grouped together by random chance, including the Earth and the human body, and therefore is all coincidental and meaningless. This also means that human consciousness exists only as a secondary effect of matter, and is generated only because of the complexity of the human brain. As well, what we believe to be a soul or Spirit is merely a delusional construct our minds created in our naive attempts to find meaning in an otherwise meaningless and pointless existence. This means that once our physical body dies, we cease to exist, forever. Materialist science, therefore, reinforces the idea that we are alone, powerless, mechanical, and that no higher intelligent forces exist. Whilst this outdated way of understanding the world is being displaced by the new revelations of quantum physics, it is still the cornerstone of the how the Cult perceives reality.

INSTITUTION 4 - BIG PHARMA AND WESTERN MEDICINE:

Estimated to be worth over a trillion dollars[10], Big Pharma, which is a name for the giant corporate multinational pharmaceutical industry, has infiltrated and corrupted western medicine. It has converted what we call medicine into a practise of poisoning with pharmaceutical drugs, and it has converted what we call doctors into glorified pharmaceutical drug pushers. The influence of Big Pharma is why, for example, medical degrees focus very little on preventive medicine—as this would limit the need for pharmaceutical drugs—and have been found in the past to only provide no more the 19.6 hours of nutritional training within their entire medical degree.[11] Big Pharma has achieved this corruption by using its immense wealth and power to influence everything from government medical policies and laws to the way universities and colleges train their doctors[12] to the way doctors treat patients. It also spends up to $30 billion dollars on public marketing alone per year, promoting its products to potential consumers.[13]

Having been heavily corrupted by Big Pharma, there are two core principles that Western medicine has built its entire foundation on that we have been programmed to assume are true, but on further investigation, reveal themselves to deeply flawed.

1. *Disease is a mostly random invasion and attack on the body, often coming from an external agent such as a germ or virus, and has very little to nothing to do with lifestyle habits.*
2. *Most healing and curing can only be achieved with the help of external agents such as pharmaceutical drugs or vaccines.*

A: TOXEMIA AND THE FALLACIOUS GERM THEORY

Many renegades in the field of alternative medicine have revealed great evidence over the last 150 years suggesting that whilst germs and viruses do exist, they are not the cause of disease, but are instead the by-products of disease. This statement will likely even surprise those with an open mind, but that is because these false beliefs have been programmed so deeply into the collective human psyche. Whilst this is a complex topic to address, I will do my best to bring clarity to this distortion, for the false programming we have received regarding the true nature of disease is very harmful.

Alternative medical research suggests that disease is actually caused by a consistent violation of the laws of Nature, which includes a largely processed, over cooked, and low nutrient dense diet, stress, toxic beliefs and thoughts, emotional suppression, a lack of exercise, fresh air, and sunshine, and an accumulation of environmental poisons. It is the toxicity that builds up in the body as a result of these factors that then creates the ideal environment for germs and viruses to feed on and multiply. This toxicity build-up is referred to as "toxemia". The late Dr. Herbert Shelton, one of the leading minds in alternative health and healing in the twentieth century, explains that, *"Toxemia is the product of fermentation and decomposition, and of the retained end products of metabolism, of worry, spite, hate, fear, jealousy, fault finding, promiscuous love, sexual excesses, overwork, overstimulation, overeating, dissipations and excesses and too much haste for the almighty dollar. The deficiencies and excesses of which the whole human race is unconsciously guilty may be properly regarded as the basic cause of disease. These are the things that enervate* (drain lifeforce energy; Author's note) *and enervation lowers functional ability. Toxemia clogs the organism, every cell, tissue, organ, nerve fibre, the blood and lymph stream, until one after another the organs of the body break down."*

The belief that germs and viruses cause disease, rather than toxemia, is something that the Big Pharma-influenced medical industry makes sure we never question. This is because as long as we believe that germs and viruses cause our illnesses, then we willingly place our blind trust in the hands of Big Pharma and consume their drugs and vaccines. This is instead of taking full responsibility for our own lifestyle choices and focusing on prevention rather than treatment.

Author Arthur M Baker explains that, *"In 1864, French chemist Louis Pasteur fathered 'The Science of Bacteriology' and 'The Germ Theory of Disease Causation' by demonstrating the existence of various micro-organisms—and concluding that these germs cause pathogenic changes in living cultures within the laboratory setting.*

"The germ theory states that diseases are due solely to invasion by specific aggressive micro-organisms. A specific germ is responsible for each disease, and micro-organisms are capable of reproduction and transportation outside of the body. With the germ theory of disease, no longer did we have to take responsibility for sickness caused by our own transgressions of the laws of health. Instead, we blamed germs that invade the body.

"The germ theory effectively shifted our personal responsibility for health and well-being onto the shoulders of the medical profession who supposedly knew how to kill off the offending germs. Our own personal health slipped from our control.

"Almost everyone in the Western world has been nurtured on the germ theory of disease: that disease is the direct consequence of the work of some outside agent, be it germ or virus."

Despite the germ theory becoming the widely accepted foundation of our modern Big Pharma-controlled medical industry, there was another theory that appeared at the same time which directly opposed it. An online article titled "The Fallacious Germ Theory" explains that, *"It was Antoine Béchamp (1816-1908), a contemporary of Pasteur, who discovered the true nature of germs. He found they were pleomorphic (capable of changing from one type of organism to another). With this theory, it is the conditions where germs live that is important (the terrain), instead of the germ itself. As Florence Nightingale put it: 'There are no specific diseases, there are specific disease conditions'.*[14]

"Pasteur himself, in one of the most quoted deathbed statements perhaps of all time, recanted the Germ Theory and admitted that his rivals had been right, and that it was not the germ that caused the disease, but rather the environment in which the germ was found: 'Bernard acail raison; le terrain c'est tout, le germe c'est rien.' He was referencing his nemesis Claude Bernard, a proponent of the Terrain Theory and contemporary of Antoine Béchamp."

Pasteur's quote on his deathbed, *"Bernard acail raison; le terrain c'est tout, le germe c'est rien"*, translates to *"Bernard was right. The microbe is nothing, the soil is everything."*[15]

Renowned scientist Dr Rudolph Virchow, who is considered the father of modern pathology and who was a vocal critic and opponent of the germ theory, said that, *"If I could live my life over again, I would devote it to proving that germs seek their natural habitat: diseased tissue, rather than being the cause of diseased tissue."*[16]

Dr. Saul Pressman explains: *"The so-called 'bad' bacteria and viruses that modern medicine fights with its huge arsenal of pharmaceutical drugs are in reality the germs of life. These germs of life live in symbiosis with the nutritive medium that constitutes our body, allowing it to be built up and later decomposed, to be metamorphosed and recreated. These germs are pleomorphic shapeshifters who are controlled by the medium in which they live.*

"Germs are not something separate, isolated, unfriendly and coming from without, but are rather the foundation for all life. Without germs, there is no life. Their number is infinite. Their function is varied. Germs can change shape, join together, separate again and return to their primordial condition. Viruses, bacteria and fungi are various developmental forms of germs. The nutritive medium on which the germs thrive determines the type of development they will undergo."[17]

The truth is that germs are not the deadly enemy of man that they have been portrayed to be, one that is attempting to invade us at any opportunity and which we must attack with all of our might. This is just something the Cult wants us to believe because it keeps us in fear, makes us feel helpless, and provides the justification to keep humanity reliant on and addicted to pharmaceutical drugs. When the body is healthy and free of toxemia, germs are actually crucial to the processes of life that build and maintain health. However, because germs are pleomorphic, when toxemia builds, they shapeshift into scavengers within the body, and could be likened to cockroaches in a rotting rubbish bin. Although, just as the cockroaches are not the cause of the rubbish that they are feeding on, neither are germs the cause of the diseased conditions that they can shapeshift to thrive in. There are trillions upon trillions of germs and bacteria within the human body, and we are breathing in or coming into contact with many thousands of others every second of the day. In fact, microscopic organisms such as bacteria, viruses, and fungi comprise more than half of the cells (57%) found in the human body.[18] Why then is everyone not permanently sick? This is because it was the "Terrain theory", proposed originally by Antoine Béchamp, that was the correct theory.

B: THE TRUE NATURE OF DISEASE

Not only are we misguided in thinking that germs and viruses are the cause of disease, but our whole understanding of the nature of disease is inverted. We have been conditioned to fear disease and treat it as something to be combatted, whereas in truth, disease is the body's attempt to initiate a *process of healing*. What we call disease is the body's attempt to heal and purge itself of the numerous poisons that have accumulated as a result of toxemia, and to heal itself of the damage those poisons have caused. It is also the body's attempt to force us to rest so that it can restore the lifeforce energy reserves that our habits have drained. Therefore, instead of attempting to "fight" disease with pharmaceutical drugs and countless other methods, all we need to do is get out of the body's way and trust in the wisdom of Nature.

Dr. Shelton explains that, "*The practice of poisoning a person because he is ill is based on erroneous notions of the essential nature of disease. In all the teachings of the medical schools, disease is regarded as something foreign to the system, as an attacking entity, and poisons are administered to war upon, drive out or destroy the enemy. But, as the truth is the exact contrary to this ancient notion, all poisoning practice is exactly wrong; it is nothing more nor less than a blind war upon the human constitution.*

"*The belief that germs can be killed inside the body is untenable, for any chemical that destroys microorganisms also destroys the body. Medical men are still trying to kill germs with drugs; the fact still remains that they damage their patients more than they do the germs.*

"*Healing is a biological process, not an art. It is as much a function of the living organism as respiration, digestion, circulation, excretion, cell proliferation, or nerve activity. It is a ceaseless process, as constant as the turning of the earth on its axis. Man can neither duplicate nor imitate nor provide a substitute for the process."*

Dr Isaac Jennings, another prominent doctor from the 1800s, explained that, *"Disease, fever, inflammation, coughs, etc., is entirely true to the laws of life, which cannot be aided by any system of medication or any medication whatever; but, relying solely upon the healing powers of the body and placing the patient in the best possible conditions for the operation of the body's own healing processes, by means of rest, fasting, diet, pure air and other Hygienic factors."*

C: SUPPRESSING THE BODY'S ATTEMPTS TO HEAL

The truth is that drugs do nothing but suppress symptoms and perform no actual healing. For example, if a person has a build-up of poisons in their stomach as a result of indulgent overeating, consuming too much alcohol, or eating spoilt food, one way the body may attempt to purge these poisons is through diarrhea and vomiting. When this occurs, we then declare ourselves to be sick and label these bodily attempts at self-cleansing and healing as a disease called "Gastro". If we consume a pharmaceutical drug that stops the diarrhea and vomiting, we believe ourselves to be "cured". The truth, however, is that we have not achieved any healing or curing at all, for all we have done is suppress the body's attempts to cleanse and heal itself. The drug itself held no magical powers and did not do anything to the body apart from adding a new poison into the system. This then forced the body to redirect its energies away from the self-healing it was undertaking (the diarrhea and vomiting), and instead focus them toward defending against the new poison. Whilst this new threat is being dealt with, we may experience temporary relief from our uncomfortable symptoms, but this is only because they have been suppressed and placed on hold. Once the drug has been combatted and expelled, the body will, if it has enough energy left, revert back to the original tasks it was performing. If this occurs, we then believe that the "disease has returned", but this is only because we mistake Nature's healing efforts to be a disease that is attacking the body.

The problem is that now the body must not only perform its original task of removing the poisons that it was attempting to purge via the diarrhea and vomiting, but it must also expel the new poison (the drug) and heal any damage that it has caused. As well, because the diarrhea and vomiting were not allowed to follow their natural course to completion, the poisons they were attempting to eject remain in the body where they can cause damage to the vital tissues and organs. This can cause more uncomfortable symptoms, which people then take even more drugs for, and they unwittingly plummet themselves into a sad and vicious cycle of never-ending symptoms and drug taking. This creates a permanent dependence upon Big Pharma, which is exactly where the Cult wants us.

INSTITUTION 5 - MODERN TECHNOLOGY:

A: PROGRAMMING THROUGH TECHNOLOGY

School is not the only way the Cult can indoctrinate its newly forming members into the ways of the Cult, as sophisticated modern technologies now allow it to shape its victims' minds in a variety of cunning ways. In the not so distant past, a child might head home from school and play in the yard or the street with their friends, building themselves a close community and learning how to interact with other people face to face. Or they might go explore Nature and spend time in solitude, learning about themselves and the world through exploration and self-discovery. When TV entered the average person's home around thirty to forty years ago, all of this changed. Rather than learning about the world through exploration and discovery, a child now had a little box with talking people on it telling them how to think, what to wear, what to buy, how to talk, what the latest trends were, who and what to fear, and what was happening in society. The education system and TV thus provided a one-two knockout punch in terms of indoctrinating the masses into the Cult. Education would teach children how not to think for themselves and to blindly trust and believe in authority, and then the TV would teach them what to think through the *programs* and authoritative sounding talking heads on the screen.

TV is well known to generate a range of alpha brainwave patterns within the viewer that induces a hypnotic like and highly suggestible state. This is why people, in particular young children, often stare at the TV like mindless zombies. In this hypnotised state, they are especially open and receptive to the messages they are receiving from the TV, as it is bypassing their paralysed conscious filters and entering straight into their subconscious mind. An online article titled "How TV influences your mind through hypnosis" explains that, *"Your mind slips into the hypnotic trance state within seconds of watching TV. This lowers your brainwaves to an 'alpha state' commonly associated with meditation and deep relaxation. This is believed to be caused by the screen flicker and explains why you feel sleepy while watching TV. Under this state of trance, your subconscious mind becomes highly suggestible and whatever information you receive from the TV becomes part of your memory pool. Since beliefs are nothing but memories, this information has the tendency to alter your beliefs or form new ones when it seeps into your subconscious mind. You might think the remote is in your hand and you're watching the programs but, in truth, you are the one who is getting programmed."*[19]

These days we have numerous technologies that can hypnotise and program the viewer in a similar fashion to TV, ranging from the large-screen cinema to smartphones, laptops, touch pads, and over the next few years we will likely be able to add more to this list. This has provided the Cult with unprecedented levels of access to the minds of its unwitting members, allowing it to program them at will.

The devastating effects this has are numerous. Rather than coming home from school and building communities, children are growing up segregated and are sitting in front of TV screens, computers, and smartphones, learning to communicate via devices and through text rather than interact in person face to face. It is lowering the attention span of people significantly and is creating addictions, as devices such as smartphones and their social media applications such as Facebook and Instagram are now well known to be highly addictive. Facebook was even shown to be deliberately modelled on how casino slot machines operate and was designed to hijack and exploit the brain's dopamine pleasure system, so that it could be more addictive to its users. Technology is also dumbing people down and encouraging them not to think anymore. Why think for yourself when the TV or Google can tell you how to think? As well, people's ability to spell and use proper grammar is diminishing because language is now being condensed into smiley face emoticons and abbreviated text, and if one can't spell a word, then never mind because their smartphone will auto-spell it for them.

Children are also losing the ability to be by themselves and enjoy solitude, ensuring they are often impatient, anxious, and constantly seeking external distractions. This is all exactly what the Cult intends, as a fragmented, dumbed down, distracted, addicted, and anxious population that cannot focus for very long or communicate with each other effectively is very easy to control.

It is not only children that are deeply affected by these technologies, but a very large portion of the adult population on Earth is also highly addicted to them now, giving the Cult unprecedented access to the minds of the masses. The most prominent industries that utilise these technologies to reach and influence our minds are Hollywood, the music industry, the pornographic industry, various multinational corporations (through marketing and advertising), and the mainstream media. All of these industries are used by the Cult to install many various programs into our minds, all of which serve its agenda.

B: CELEBRITY WORSHIP

Hollywood and the music industry, along with the mainstream media, perform the role of instilling the concept of celebrity worship into the minds of the masses by encouraging them to place other, more famous and privileged Cult members on a pedestal. This causes them to think that these people are more important and powerful than everyone else simply because of how much money they make and how popular their movies and music are. Big corporate brands then capitalize on their celebrity influence over the masses by using them to help them sell their products and to set new public trends. The influence that these celebrities have over the worshipping Cult masses, combined with big budget marketing campaigns, subsequently has a major impact on how people think, what people wear, what brands they purchase, what technology they use, how they speak and interact, what hairstyle they adopt, and what body shape they believe is acceptable, just to name a few.

Celebrity worship can lead the average person to feel disempowered and insignificant, and that just being themselves is not good enough. This causes them to think that they need to pursue money and celebrity status in order to be loved and accepted, which is a mindset that young and impressionable children and teenagers are particularly susceptible to.

Many celebrities also rely upon sexual exploitation to generate their fame as it is well known that sex sells, and as a result, Hollywood and the music industry place a major priority on youthfulness, beauty, and producing highly sexually suggestive material. Most celebrities now rely on plastic surgery, botox, photoshopping, and other methods in order to keep up with these demands so that they can stay popular and relevant. This suggests to the other members of the Cult that if they want to be accepted and loved by others, they must seek eternal beauty, and must be sexually enticing to others.

One cunning deception Hollywood in particular helps to generate is to make the madness of the Cult appear "normal". When we see famous celebrities acting like "everyday" people and doing "everyday" Cult things in movies, TV programs, and the media, the subliminal message we receive is *"see, even celebrities do not question the way Cult-life is or their position within the Cult. This is all just normal, stop asking questions and go back to sleep"*. The truth, however, is that they are performers playing a role, and most are getting paid incredible amounts of money to do so. As a result, their lives are nothing like the rest of the "non privileged" Cult members. The reason the Cult allows these people to have so much money and celebrity status is not because it cares about them and wants them to have nice and luxurious lives; it is because they play such an important role in making the Cult appear normal and sane to the programmed masses. People who are actually trying to make a hands-on difference within the Cult, such as nurses, teachers, volunteers and so on, are not even paid 1% of what many celebrities receive. This is because the Cult is not designed or structured to reward those helping others, but is designed to reward those reinforcing the power and control of the Cult. This of course is not taking away from any celebrities who sincerely attempt to use their influence and wealth to help the masses, but these are generally the exceptions rather than the rule. As well, generally what they are helping to solve or support are issues created by the Cult. Whereas any celebrity who attempts to get to the source of the problem and help the masses break free from their hypnosis, will have their public image and reputation ridiculed and destroyed by the Cult's mainstream media.

INSTITUTION 6 - MAINSTREAM MEDIA:

The mainstream media (MSM) are what help to create the culture of celebrity-worshipping within the Cult, but also play many other roles. One role, as mentioned above, is to ensure that these celebrities do not use their influence to awaken the masses out of their trance. It achieves this by maintaining control over the public's opinion regarding each celebrity, as this gives it the power to give or take away the highly respected status that they enjoy. More specifically, it generates stories and headlines about celebrities that portray them as either heroes or villains. Not only is this entertaining for the Cult masses and thus good for ratings and sales, but it also ensures that the celebrities are always on their best behaviour. They learn very quickly that the "good behaviour" expected of them by the Cult means helping to keep the masses asleep and not questioning their position, whereas "bad behaviour" means trying to awaken or help the masses become free from the Cult in any way.

One way that the MSM convert a celebrity into a public villain is by creating and spreading headlines, stories, and photos that make the celebrity appear as if they have gone crazy or are having a mental breakdown. Or they will spread pure, blatant lies about this person in order to discredit their character and make them look stupid, insensitive, and corrupt. When the MSM publicly attack and shame celebrities in this manner, they are saying to the masses, *"Let this be an example of what will happen to you if you ever dare step out of line!"* To the other Cult celebrities, they are saying, *"Here is an example of how we will destroy your reputation and career if you dare attempt to awaken and free the masses."* As a result, the MSM function like a security guard at a gate, not allowing anyone to leave their confinement.

When a celebrity plays within the rules, however, and helps to reinforce the Cult's programming over the masses, the media will portray him or her as an upstanding citizen, and possibly even a hero. Once again, the message to the masses is clear: *"You will avoid the Cult's condemnation only if you conform to and remain obedient to the Cult."* To the other celebrities, it says, *"This is the type of behaviour you must demonstrate if you wish to maintain your reputation and privileges."*

The MSM also have the "important" task of informing us about what is happening in the world of the Cult through daily news updates. The true purpose of this, however, is to keep the Cult members hypnotised and in a constant state of fear, anxiety, and division. It achieves this by continuously presenting narrative and content that is highly negative, divisive, and fear inducing.

On the odd occasion a major story will break that threatens to expose the Cult and those controlling it; in this scenario the MSM will function as a tool for the Cult to control the public's perceptions around that story's narrative. This is achieved by presenting an "official" statement in the media from an important looking "authority" (often a politician), and then using extracts from this statement to generate headlines and slogans. These headlines and slogans are then repeated again and again and again in the media, and are often accompanied by images and stories that make this authority appear trustworthy and respectable. Often this "official" statement and the ensuing headlines and slogans are full of blatant lies, but this does not matter, for the purpose is not to reveal the truth but to deflect people's attention away from the truth. The use of repetitive headlines and slogans is very effective, as it pummels the message so deep into people's subconscious minds that they don't even think to question what they are being told. The goal of the MSM is to make people assume that *"this (insert lie) is just what happened, everyone knows that!"*. This deception is repeated again and again and eventually leads to a population of people whose perceptions and beliefs about the world are built upon a complex and dense web of lies. All of which must be unravelled bit by bit if one is to free themselves from the Cult.

Despite its best efforts to deceive, some lies within the MSM do eventually come undone, and so to counteract this, the MSM will attack and discredit anyone challenging the official narrative that they have been spruiking. Or, on the very rare occasion that the masses don't fall for the MSM's mind programming tricks, they will simply divert people's attention toward another story by generating new and unrelated headlines. Eventually, most people will simply forget about the old story and move on.[20]

INSTITUTION 7 - SOCIAL MEDIA:

With the concept of celebrity worship deeply installed, the Cult has provided its members with the opportunity to emulate their celebrity gods by trying to become just like them. This opportunity has been provided by the digital platforms known as social media, in particular Facebook, Twitter, and Instagram. What this has led to is an unprecedented explosion of selfie-taking narcissism and self-obsession as the masses desperately seek fame, popularity, attention, and recognition.

Social media also provide more platforms and extra reach for the MSM to continue with its roles mentioned above. On top of this, social media have provided the perfect platforms for the Cult to deeply study the masses through data mining. This is possible because people are constantly uploading nearly everything they are doing every moment of the day onto their social media pages. This includes what they're eating, where they're going, what they're talking about, who they associate with, what they like and dislike, what their beliefs are, and what their fears are. Even when social media engines aren't being used directly, they still have easy backdoor access to everything a person is doing through their smart devices. Data such as this are crucial as it can be used to better understand and thus program the minds of the masses.

Social media also ensure that people are very rarely living in the present moment, because they are too distracted by constantly displaying, sharing, and comparing every part of their lives with everyone else. On top of this, as mentioned previously, social media have been well proven to have been designed to be highly addictive, to shorten attention spans, and has led to a major increase in cyberbullying.[21]

INSTITUTION 8 - THE BANKING SYSTEM:

A: CONTROL THE MONEY, CONTROL THE CULT

There was once a time in the past where human activities and interactions were not dictated solely by money. Along with using money, it was also common for humans to trade and barter between each other, and this could include trading goods or even skills. For example, if one person was a skilled baker, and another was a skilled carpenter, the baker might trade some loaves of bread in return for the carpenter repairing something for him. Therefore, one's status and importance within society was not just determined by how much money one had, but also by one's skills, character, and integrity.

In contrast, these days money now dictates just about everything. This includes someone's status and standing within the Cult, how much time and freedom they have, how many luxuries they can afford, and how much power and influence they have over others. Put simply, money now controls the Cult on every level imaginable, which means that those who control the money control the Cult.

Certain "elite" members of the Rothschild dynasty, along with other elite aristocratic families, have manoeuvred themselves into positions of unimaginable global economic power through their control over the central banks. A central bank is an institution that manages and controls the money supply, currency, and interest rates of a nation, and in each country that has one installed, which is nearly every country in the world, it is known as the Federal Reserve Bank (FRB). However, these elite families have also created and control the *world central banks* such as the European Central

Bank, the International Monetary Fund, and the World Bank. Through these central banks, the rulers of the Cult have been able to cripple each country's economy by deliberately engineering inflation, debt, and various economic crashes, which they can then exploit by taking over each country's government and all of their major industries. How this is done exactly is explained in methodical detail in the book *The Creature from Jekyll Island* by G. Edward Griffin. This has led us to the point where only 1% of people on the planet now own half the world's wealth, and this divide between the super wealthy and the rest is growing by the day, for the 1% have the entire planet's wealth in their sights.[22]

What these elite bankers rely on is the public's ignorance regarding how the FRB in each country actually works and not realising that the FRB isn't a government-created institution, but is a privately created one that serves private interests only. This is why when it was created, they used the title "Federal Reserve Bank" rather than the more accurate title of "Central Bank", as this gives it the illusion of being an official government-regulated entity. Regardless, since its creation, it has developed so much power and influence that it now basically creates and follows its own rules and operates outside of the jurisdiction of government.

B: ENGINEERING INFLATION

Engineering inflation through the central banks is one of the biggest weapons the Cult uses to cripple and control each nation. This is achieved by the FRB allowing each bank to practise what is known as "fractional reserve banking", which gives the banks the power to create and loan money that doesn't exist. Most people don't realise that when they go into a bank to receive a large loan, that bank doesn't actually have that money; the bank simply types it up onto a screen and then transfers it into their account. This is a simplified version of how it works, but it is the basic premise of fractional reserve banking. Inflation is also created by the FRB's ability to print as much paper money as they like out of thin air, even if it is not backed by anything real and tangible like gold and silver. What then occurs is that the economy becomes *inflated* with so much money circulating, via credit loans and unbacked paper money, that the value of money goes down. Then, because money is less valuable, its purchasing power is decreased and more of it is needed in order to purchase goods, which creates a rise in prices, or what we call inflation.

Inflation has meant that the purchasing power of a dollar today has greatly diminished in value compared to what it was in the past. This has led to the costs of daily living rising dramatically, especially the cost of larger purchases such as a house, which forces people to take out large loans, locking them down in debt. On top of this, not only can banks provide these loans by creating money out of thin air, but they can also charge interest on them, meaning that they are nearly impossible to pay back. As a result of having to pay back loans along with interest, and living in a perpetually inflating economy, most people are then forced to become locked into the 9 to 5 work system just to keep their heads above water. Or alternatively, people are forced to work multiple jobs. This means that they are forced to spend about one-third of their precious time on this planet doing what are often menial and mind-numbing tasks in order to avoid being crushed by debt. To make things even more difficult, they are also forced to surrender a solid portion of their hard-earned money to various taxes under the threat of being thrown in a cage.[23] This is all very much by design, as the Cult wants us like hamsters trapped on a spinning wheel that we can't get off, locked in survival mode and in a constant state of stress, fear, and tension.

Michael Tellinger, the author of *UBUNTU Contributionism*, summed the situation up well when he said, "*The creation and supply of money lies in the hands of a few families, mainly the Rothschild, Rockefeller, Morgan, Carnegie, Harriman, Schiff, Warburg and a handful of others.*

"*These incredibly powerful families control the entire planet's money supply. They have the right to print and distribute money without restriction. Their rights are protected by the current governments of the world and the military might that upholds the governments. These are further supported by the laws that are made by the governments and the courts that uphold such laws. All of this activity is kept nice and tidy under control of the banking elite who in turn keep the governments in power.*

"*It is a system so skilfully crafted that we have to admire its architects for keeping us in the dark for so long. But now that we have figured out that we are mere pawns in a huge game of global slavery, it is time for change.*"

C: A PERFORMANCE REVIEW OF THE FEDERAL RESERVE BANK

On the website of the Federal Reserve Bank of America, they claim that, "*The Federal Reserve, the central bank of the United States, provides the nation with a safe, flexible, and stable monetary and financial system.*"

However, in his book *The Creature from Jekyll Island*, G Edward Griffin gives a more realistic account, and whilst he is referring to America, what he is saying can be applied to any country controlled by a FRB. "*The accepted version of history is that the Federal Reserve was created to stabilize our economy. One of the most widely used textbooks on this subject says: "It sprang from the panic of 1907, with its alarming epidemic of bank failures: the country was fed up once and for all with the anarchy of unstable private banking."*

"Even the most naive student must sense a grave contradiction between this cherished view, and the System's actual performance. Since its inception, it has presided over the crashes of 1921 and 1929, the Great Depression of '29 to '39, recessions in '53, '57, '69, '75, and '81; a stock market 'Black Monday' in '87; and a 1000% inflation which has destroyed 90% of the dollar's purchasing power (as well as the 2008 crash that happened after Griffin's book was written; Author's note).

"Let us be more specific on that last point. By 1990, an annual income of $10,000 was required to buy what took only $1000 in 1914. That incredible loss in value was quietly transferred to the federal government in the form of hidden taxation, and the Federal Reserve System was the mechanism by which it was accomplished. Actions have consequences. The consequences of 'wealth confiscation' by the Federal-Reserve mechanisms are now upon us. In the current decade, corporate debt is soaring; personal debt is greater than ever; both business and personal bankruptcies are at an all-time high; banks and savings and loans associations are failing in larger numbers than ever before; interest on the national debt is consuming half of our tax dollars; heavy industry largely has been replaced by overseas competitors; we are facing an international trade deficit for the first time in our history; 75% of downtown Los Angeles and other metropolitan areas is owned by foreigners, and over half of our nation is in a state of economic recession.

"That is the scorecard eighty years after the Federal Reserve was created supposedly to stabilize our economy! There can be no argument that the System has failed in its stated objectives. Furthermore, after all this time, after repeated changes in personnel, after operating under both political parties, after numerous experiments in monetary philosophy, after almost a hundred revisions to its charter, and after the development of countless new formulas and techniques, there has been more than ample opportunity to work out mere procedural flaws.

"It is not unreasonable to conclude, therefore, that the System has failed, not because it needs a new set of rules or more intelligent directors, but because it is incapable of achieving its stated objectives.

"If an institution is incapable of achieving its objectives, there is no reason to preserve it–unless it can be altered in some way to change its capability. That leads to the question: why is the System incapable of achieving its stated objectives? The painful answer is: those were never its true objectives. When one realizes the circumstances under which it was created, when one contemplates the identities of those who authored it, and when one studies its actual performance over the years, it becomes obvious that the System is merely a cartel with a government facade. There is no doubt that those who run it are motivated to maintain full employment, high productivity, low inflation, and a generally sound economy. They are not interested in killing the goose that lays such beautiful golden eggs. But, when there is a conflict between the public interest and the private needs of the cartel–a conflict that arises almost daily–the public will be sacrificed. That is the nature of the beast. It is foolish to expect a cartel to act in any other way."

The banking elite have also had a major hand in setting up the structure of the education system, and this is why no one is taught exactly how the FRB and fractional reserve banking system truly works. Meanwhile, the Cult's elite teach their children exactly how the game works, and how to become the next generation of elite who manipulate and exploit the masses just like those before them.

INSTITUTION 9 – BIG FOOD CORPORATIONS:

We now live in a world dominated by corporate food giants who fill the supermarket aisles with processed junk food that is nutritionally dead and toxic to the body. Because these corporate giants are so large and are backed by so much money, they can spend millions of dollars on global marketing campaigns to promote their foods and get their brands deeply embedded into the subconscious minds of the masses. Their methods of achieving this are highly varied, from becoming sponsors of sporting teams, using TV adverts and billboards, to being shown on-screen in popular movies, music clips, and TV shows. The most insidious of all, however, is when these big food giants launch marketing campaigns targeted at children. Children have not yet developed the ability to discern good from bad and healthy from unhealthy, and they are subsequently very easy to manipulate. Marketers of big food companies understand that if they can create strong emotional attachments to their products in children, then they will likely create valuable and loyal consumers for life. As well, junk foods are designed to hijack the body's senses in artificial ways and produce drug-like effects within the brain. This means that they are literally addictive, and because the goal of these corporate giants is simply to expand their power and profits, any addicted customer to them is a good customer. For the average person, what this means is that they can find themselves in adulthood with many addictions to different foods and subsequent health problems that were generated in a period of their lives when they weren't even fully conscious. What makes these foods even more tantalizing is that they become emotional suppressants for many people, who use them to cope with living in the stressful and out of balance world that is created by the Cult.

2: IN SUMMARY

The following is a summary of all of the issues we may be facing when we reach adulthood as a result of being raised in a negative family environment, along with all of the Cult-based institutions previously mentioned:

- *Feeling unloved and unlovable and carrying unconscious traumas from childhood.*
- *Carrying unconscious beliefs such as "I am not worthy", "I am not loveable", "My body is shameful", "I am dumb", "I will never achieve anything", "I must conform to be accepted", etc.*
- *Seeing the world through a distorted left-brain perspective, disconnected from the body's intelligence and from Spirit.*
- *Heavily conditioned to believe in, be fearful of, seek approval from, and be completely obedient to authority.*
- *Believing we live in a mostly competitive rather than cooperative world.*
- *Filled with rigid dead knowledge, rather than evolving living knowledge.*
- *Believing we are an inferior being and that every action we perform is being judged by a personalised God that is external from us.*
- *Feeling guilt and shame about our body and in particular about our sexuality.*

- *Lacking any true knowledge about disease, health and healing, and are reliant upon (and likely addicted to) pharmaceutical drugs.*
- *Blindly following trends set by celebrities and believing that beauty and youthfulness make one person better than another.*
- *Adopting a fear-based perspective of the world as a result of our mainstream media programming.*
- *Highly narcissistic and self-obsessed, especially on social media.*
- *Addicted to social media and technologies like smartphones.*
- *Suffering from a poor attention span.*
- *Driven by a fear of poverty and being crippled by debt.*
- *Addicted to junk foods and products, and subsequently at high risk of diseases such as obesity, heart disease, and cancer.*
- *Suffering from Stockholm Syndrome that makes us love and defend our servitude within the Cult.*

CHAPTER 5:

THE SHADOW

1: OUR SUPPRESSED DARK SIDE

The early life and institutional programming that we all receive, ensures that most people live their entire lives within the Cult falsely identified with their body and ego personality as being their true self. As well as being disconnected from the higher guidance of Spirit. This has become so normalised that very few people ever question the mechanical and unconscious nature of modern human life, with nearly everyone hiding behind carefully constructed social masks to conceal their fear of being authentic. Rarely is success and fulfilment determined by who can be the most authentic, creative, original, and supportive of others. It is instead determined by who can best conform to the Cult's corrupted values and ideologies, and who can best prey on their fellow man to reach the top of the societal pecking order. As per the nature of the law of the jungle.

Even many personal development and spiritual teachers who teach others how to be more "successful and happy" often do not teach how to awaken the true self, but instead teach how to better craft one's social masks and adapt to life in the Cult. This may allow one to be more successful in a conventional sense, such as achieving more money, material possessions, and popularity and influence, or it may provide a false sense of happiness by programming one's mind with hypnotising spiritual clichés, but it will not help one to awaken and become truly free. This is not to say that creating a more comfortable life for ourselves is not beneficial in any way, for it is better than living a life of constant hardship, but it is not true freedom. Instead, it could be likened to creating a more comfortable prison cell within our captivity. Hiding behind social masks in our day-to-day lives fragments our ego personality and creates what is known as the unconscious "shadow", a term coined by the late renowned psychologist Carl Jung. Jung explained that the shadow archetype is the part of ourselves that contains all of the traits and behaviours that we have learned from a young age aren't "appropriate" or socially acceptable to express. This particularly includes qualities that may bring us judgment, criticism, and disapproval from others, such as expressing our fears, anger, hurt, sadness, grief, wounds, traumas, and limiting beliefs. It also includes what could be recognised as more positive suppressed traits and emotions such as creative gifts, talents, and ideas, natural sexual impulses, and other passions and desires. We then live our lives hidden behind contrived social masks, which we mistake to be authentic, and which cause us to believe that just because they present an image of happiness, success, confidence, and purity to the world that these qualities define our identity. The truth, however, is that behind these masks, down in the suppressed shadow, lie many of the exact opposite traits.

Joseph Campbell explained that, *"There's a lot in you that's neither being carried into this persona system nor into your ego, as part of what you perceive as 'you.' Just opposite to the ego, buried in the unconscious, is what Jung calls the shadow.*

"Now, the society (the Cult; Author's note) *will give you a role to play, and this means that you've got to cut out of your life many of the things that you, as a person, might think or do. These potentials get shunted down into the unconscious. Your society tells you, 'You should do this, you should do that,' but it also says, 'You mustn't do this, you mustn't do the other thing.' Those things you'd like to do, which are really not very nice things to want to do, those get placed down in the unconscious, too. This is the centre of the personal unconscious*

"The shadow is, so to say, the blind spot in your nature. It's that which you won't look at about yourself. This is the counterpart exactly of the Freudian unconscious, the repressed recollections as well as the repressed potentialities in you.

"The shadow is that which you might have been had you been born on the other side of the tracks: the other person, the other you. It is made up of the desires and ideas within you that you are repressing—all of the introjected id. The shadow is the landfill of the self. Yet it is also a sort of vault: it holds great, unrealized potentialities within you.

"The nature of your shadow is a function of the nature of your ego. It is the backside of your light side. In the myths, the shadow is represented as the monster that has to be overcome, the dragon. It is the dark thing that comes up from the abyss and confronts you the minute you begin moving down into the unconscious. It is the thing that scares you so that you don't want to go down there. It knocks from below. Who's that down there? Who's that up there? This is all very, very mysterious and frightening.

"If your personal role is too thin, too narrow—if you've buried too much of yourself within your shadow—you're going to dry up. Most of your energies are not available to you. A lot can get gathered there in the depths. And eventually, enantiodromia (a complete shift; Author's note) *is going to hit, and that unrecognized, unheeded demon is going to come roaring up into the light.*

"The shadow is the part of you that you don't know is there. Your friends see it, however, and it's also why some people don't like you. The shadow is you as you might have been; it is that aspect of you which might have been if you had allowed yourself to fulfill your unacceptable potential.

"Society, of course, does not recognize these aspects of your potential self. You are not recognizing these aspects of yourself either; you don't know that they're there or that you have repressed them. The shadow is that part of you that you won't allow to show through, that includes good—I mean potent—as well as dangerous and disastrous aspects of your potential."[24]

Carl Jung himself explained, *"The situation which is more common and more familiar to the average man is that in which the ego identifies itself with the ethical values. The identification takes place by means of an identification of the ego with the persona* (social mask; Author's note). *The ego confuses itself with the façade personality (which is of course in reality only that part of the personality that is tailored to fit the collective), and forgets that it possesses aspects which run counter to the persona. This means that the ego has repressed the shadow side and lost touch with the dark contents, which are negative and for this reason split off from the conscious sector."*[25]

The journey of awakening and connecting back to the true self is not about suppressing or ignoring the perceived negative qualities within us, but about confronting and coming to awareness and acceptance of them, allowing us to integrate the shadow back into the ego personality. This integration of the shadow is what many refer to as *shadow work*, which empowers us to be wholly authentic to who we are. If we do not pursue shadow work, then we remain unconsciously trapped behind false masks, and the shadow becomes self-destructive and drains our lifeforce and potential.

Jung again explains that, *"When one tries desperately to be good and wonderful and perfect, then all the more the shadow develops a definite will to be black and evil and destructive. People cannot see that; they are always striving to be marvellous, and then they discover that terrible destructive things happen which they cannot understand, and they either deny that such facts have anything to do with them, or if they admit them, they take them for natural afflictions, or they try to minimize them and to shift the responsibility elsewhere.*

"The fact is that if one tries beyond one's capacity to be perfect, the shadow descends into hell and becomes the devil. For it is just as sinful from the standpoint of nature and of truth to be above oneself as to be below oneself.

"It is surely not the divine will in man that he should be something which he is not, for when one looks into nature, one sees that it is most definitely the divine will that everything should be what it is."

2: SHADOW PROJECTION

A major blockage to pursuing sincere shadow work is something known as "shadow projection". Shadow projection occurs when we project judgment and criticism toward another person or group that represents certain qualities that we have supressed in ourselves, and is often accompanied by feelings of intense anger and indignation. For example, we may have been raised to believe that we must always be nice, polite, and kind to other people. This is a nice set of values to adopt, but it may also cause us to fear any interactions that are confrontational, because we deem them as rude and inconsiderate. Then, when we come into contact with someone who isn't afraid of confrontation, they will inevitably trigger this fear within us. What happens next in the case of shadow projection is that we project our unconscious fear onto the other person in the form of judgment, criticism, and anger. This is because they are acting in a way that we ourselves have deemed to be socially unacceptable, so we then project that judgment onto their behaviour as well, considering it rude and inconsiderate. This might even be the case if this person hasn't done anything directly rude or inconsiderate toward us.

The anger and indignation this person triggers in us actually present a valuable opportunity to look within and confront our suppressed shadow, but if we instead shadow project, we divert all of the responsibility for how we feel onto the other person, and we miss this opportunity. Sincere shadow work demands that we resist the temptation to shadow project, and instead sit with and confront our uncomfortable emotions, as well as inquire as to what part of ourselves they have arisen from. In the example above, this provides an opportunity for us to learn to become okay and comfortable with confrontation when it is required, for confrontation allows us to set healthy and firm boundaries to avoid being exploited by others.

Shadow projection can even display itself within the collective psyche of a large group of people. An example of this is a country that acquires a president that many people hate because they perceive him as being greedy, narcissistic, and ego driven. Whilst this person may indeed embody those traits, the hatred and judgment that he triggers in others is because he represents the very same suppressed traits within the collective shadow of the people in that country. However, rather than admit and confront this reality with self-honesty, the public can instead project all of the blame for how they feel back onto the president, thus shifting the need to take responsibility for their own shadow.

By understanding the shadow and avoiding the temptation to shadow project, we not only increase our self-awareness and become more authentic, but an immense amount of conflict and drama within personal relationships and the world can be avoided. What helps in the process of shadow work significantly is the awakening of the true self. The true self is observing life from an expanded point of awareness, and can see both the conscious and shadow aspects of our ego. Therefore, it has the power to simply observe its conditioning and unconscious emotional reactions without reacting or projecting them.

Carl Jung explains, *"If you imagine someone who is brave enough to withdraw all his projections, then you get an individual who is conscious of a pretty thick shadow. Such a man has saddled himself with new problems and conflicts. He has become a serious problem to himself, as he is now unable to say that they do this or that, they are wrong, and they must be fought against. He lives in the House of the Gathering. Such a man knows that whatever is wrong in the world is in himself, and if he only learns to deal with his own shadow, he has done something real for the world. He has succeeded in shouldering at least an infinitesimal part of the gigantic, unsolved social problems of our day."*

CHAPTER 6

SPIRITUAL EMBODIMENT

Spiritual embodiment is the process of awakening and reconnecting to one's Spirit and then anchoring it in the body. This allows Spirit to become expressed through the body and ego personality, thus becoming actualised in the physical world. Whereas, until this occurs, the body and ego personality remain in charge, and concepts such as "Spirit and soul" are little more than abstract obscurities within the mind.

Through Spiritual embodiment, all of the false "I's" of the body and ego personality are gradually unified and placed in service to Spirit. This results in our earthly mission transforming from being driven by surviving within the law of the jungle, to being driven and fuelled by the will of Spirit. Outwardly, a spiritually embodied person may appear normal, but inwardly they will have experienced a profound and life-changing shift, as their awareness has greatly expanded. The Cult architects understand our potential for Spiritual embodiment, which they know will cause us to seek deeper answers of a more esoteric nature, eventually allowing us to become aware of the prison we are in. This means that a collective embodied spiritual awakening is a direct threat to their power and control. Therefore, to counteract this, the entire Cult is designed to keep us spiritually disembodied, and believing that concepts such as Spirit and soul are nothing more than intangible and naive myths and superstitions.

This is why the Cult herds us into the education system as early as possible, as it is designed to initiate the disembodiment process in those pivotal early years when the connection between Spirit, body, and ego personality is being formed. As mentioned previously, the education system teaches us to live solely in the head and disconnects us from the body's intelligence, which disconnects us from the voice of Spirit.

1: DISEMBODIMENT

Disembodiment begins as children learn to develop rigid patterns of tension within the body whenever they encounter stress or trauma. These patterns of tension are defensive mechanisms against stress and trauma, as they help to alleviate our fear and anxiety, and to suppress any bodily urges that may get us into trouble. This is why education, and Cult life in general, is designed to expose us to intense stress and trauma as early as possible, as well as place us in environments that do not allow our bodily urges to be expressed naturally. As children, our natural instincts are to play and explore, and to allow emotions and other sensations to move through our bodies with unbridled enthusiasm and creative expression; this is how we learn about ourselves and the world. In school, and in Cult life in general, we are constantly placed in situations whereby our natural urges must be suppressed, for they can get us in trouble and lead to punishment. Or, we are constantly told that certain emotions and urges that we are expressing are "bad" and "unacceptable", which can cause us to feel shame and embarrassment about ourselves. As a result, we begin judging our natural urges as "wrong", which causes us stress and anxiety when they arise, and leads us to unconsciously suppress them by tensing the body and restricting the breath. This unconscious tension then causes the centre of our awareness to retract out of the body and up into the head, and once up in the head we become desensitised to the body's sensations. This temporarily numbs our stress and anxiety; however, as mentioned, it also desensitises us to the body's intelligence and therefore to the voice of Spirit, which is exactly where the Cult wants us.

When we encounter stress as children, it is most common to develop unconscious tension in areas such as the abdomen, chest, neck, jaw, and face, and to restrict our breathing so that it becomes shallow. If we are exposed to stress regularly, which happens to nearly everyone within the Cult, then our unconscious tension becomes a habit that is performed repeatedly. This repetition then creates deep wiring within the nervous system that causes our tension to become permanent. This results in the centre of our awareness also retracting permanently from the body and residing itself solely up in the head, where our desensitisation to the body's intelligence becomes normalised and familiar.

Therefore, in order for our Spiritual embodiment process to be effective, we must become aware of the specific patterns of unconscious tension that we have learned to habitually hold, and then learn to slowly rewire these habits one by one. At the same time as consciously becoming more in tune with the body's subtle energies and sensations. The only way to rewire deeply ingrained habits is through first becoming aware of exactly where in the body they are being exhibited, and then by relaxing these areas through conscious willpower whenever the habit arises. If we can maintain this conscious self-vigilance repeatedly over a long enough period, our habits will begin to rewire within the nervous system and will be replaced with new ones. This then allows the centre of our awareness to slowly drop out of the head and back down into the body, and we become re-sensitised to the body's intelligence, and thus to the voice of Spirit.

2: THE BODY-BRAIN

Let's now look more deeply into the concept of the *body's intelligence*.

We have been so deeply conditioned to have the centre of our awareness residing permanently in the head, and to perceive the head-brain as the solitary master of the body, that very few people realise that there exist two other brains within the body. These are the brain in the heart and the brain in the gut. I am not just talking figuratively here, as modern neuroscience is confirming that both of these regions literally contain nervous systems complex enough to be considered brains, with each brain containing its own strengths and unique style of intelligence.

In regard to the heart, the HeartMath Institute, which has been studying the heart-brain for nearly thirty years, explains that, "*Traditionally, the study of communication pathways between the head and heart has been approached from a rather one-sided perspective, with scientists focusing primarily on the heart's responses to the brain's commands. We have learned, however, that communication between the heart and brain actually is a dynamic, ongoing, two-way dialogue, with each organ continuously influencing the other's function. Research has shown that the heart communicates to the brain in four major ways: neurologically (through the transmission of nerve impulses), biochemically (via hormones and neurotransmitters), biophysically (through pressure waves) and energetically (through electromagnetic field interactions). Communication along all these conduits significantly affects the brain's activity.*

"The heart-brain, as it is commonly called, or intrinsic cardiac nervous system, is an intricate network of complex ganglia, neurotransmitters, proteins, and support cells, the same as those of the brain in the head. The heart-brain's neural circuitry enables it to act independently of the cranial brain to learn, remember, make decisions and even feel and sense."

The HeartMath Institute has even discovered that there are more neural pathways passing from the heart-brain to the head-brain than there are the other way around. They explain that, *"In terms of heart-brain communication, it is generally well known that the efferent (descending) pathways in the autonomic nervous system are involved in the regulation of the heart. However, it is less appreciated that the majority of fibers in the vagus nerves are afferent (ascending) in nature. Furthermore, more of these ascending neural pathways are related to the heart (and cardiovascular system) than to any other organ. This means the heart sends more information to the brain than the brain sends to the heart."*[26]

In regard to the gut-brain, Philip Shepherd explains in his book *Radical Wholeness* that the science of neurogastroenterology (a branch of neuroscience focused on the gut-brain) has found that the brain in the gastrointestinal tract can function independently even when the brain is vegetative. He explains that, *"On its own, it thinks, perceives, remembers, decides and acts—and creates 95 percent of the body's serotonin, a neurotransmitter that helps regulate mood, appetite, and sleep. The functioning of this second brain also affects memory, learning, decision making, anxiety, and depression. It has been linked to autism, Parkinson's, and Alzheimer's. An article on the Harvard Medical School website notes that 'the brain and the gastrointestinal (GI) system are intimately connected – so intimately that they should be viewed as one system.'"*[27]

There is also a great deal of research to suggest that the microbiome bacteria in the gut play a major role in our thinking and behaviour.[28]

The spiritual embodiment process requires that we cease identifying with the head-brain as the solitary master brain of the body, and instead allow ourselves to become sensitised to and informed by all three brains together. In truth, they are not even three different brains, but are three focal points of one *entire body-brain*. Therefore, this concept demands a complete reassociation of what we are speaking of when we refer to "the brain". Normally when people speak of the brain, they are referring only to the head-brain, but a more accurate statement would be to refer to the *body-brain*, with its three main focal points being the head, heart, and belly. Understandably, due to the fact that the concept of the head-brain being the solitary master brain is so deeply embedded into the human psyche, it will be a while before this association begins to change on a collective scale.

3: THE INNER MALE AND FEMALE

The body's intelligence as a whole contains two prime elements, one being male and the other being female (or masculine and feminine), and both of these elements provide their own unique strengths and ways of perceiving the world. However, it is important to note that this has nothing to do with human gender as both sexes—men and women—have these two elements within them.

The centre of awareness of the male element sits within the head-brain whereas the centre of awareness of the female element sits within the gut-brain down in the lower belly. An embodied individual has both of these elements existing in harmony and union, allowing them to utilise both of their strengths and unique types of intelligence. Whereas, those who are disembodied live exclusively up in the head-brain, with the intelligence of the male element dominating their perceptions of the world.

The male element thinks in terms of logic, reason, hierarchy, division, abstraction, linear time, and is highly wilful. He seeks to label the world and break it up in to familiar and comforting categories that he understands, and he becomes anxious when something is not within his control. His intelligence is associated with the ego personality and is the type of intelligence that the Cult programs us to identify with. In contrast, the intelligence of the female element thinks in terms of wholeness, connection, feeling, sensitivity, and intuition. She does not seek to label and compartmentalise the world, as she accepts it as it is without judgment, and surrenders to its mystery. She is our direct link with Spirit, and therefore a spiritually embodied person is led by her guidance, with the male element operating as her faithful servant.

When in union with his female counterpart, the intelligence of the male element is softened, balanced, and enriched with wisdom, and expresses qualities such as strength, honour, nobility, logic, reason, focus, and resilience. Unfortunately, as a result of dissociating from the body and living up in our head, most of us have desensitised ourselves to the intelligence and guidance of the female element. Without the crucial balance of his female counterpart, the male element then transforms into the archetype of the male tyrant, which again, has nothing to do with gender, for both men and women can and do embody the male tyrant.

4: THE MALE TYRANT

Detached from the female's connection to Wholeness, the tyrant sees the world as a place of division and hierarchy. A world in which those higher up on the pecking order have the right to exploit and control those below. He is particularly interested in climbing this pecking order and being the one on top.

Having been cut off from Spirit, which is his connection to the eternal, he also deeply fears death. Therefore, his main drive in life is to achieve physical immortality. The fact that this is impossible does not matter, for the tyrant does not see reality through a clear and rational lens, as he is blinded by his fears, ambitions, and wishful thinking.

In the past, those who have embodied the tyrant have strived for immortality through endless conquest and power over others. Through their achievements, they ensure their names are etched in stone, written into the record books, and their images captured in statues. If their physical bodies could not continue, then they at least had to ensure that their names and legacies were never forgotten, even if that legacy left behind nothing but death and destruction. These days, the tyrant actually believes he can eventually achieve immortality through what is known as 'transhumanism'. This is the belief that disease, ageing, and even death can be conquered by introducing robotics and artificial intelligence into the body, which is something I will discuss in more depth in Chapter 15.

Because the tyrant is fuelled by fear, he is prone to suffering from chronic paranoia and insecurity, and to appease these feelings he is always looking for ways to feel more secure about his position in the world. The way he seeks security is via obtaining power and control over others, as well as through the acquisition of material possessions. However, he finds that these pursuits never succeed in alleviating his suffering, as its true cause lies in his disconnection from Spirit.

Despite his futile attempts to obtain security, the tyrant's appetite for control and material possessions only grows more and more insatiable. We see this insatiable appetite for security embodied by the giant multinational corporations of the world who seek to crush all competition and create a monopoly of control in their field. Or, by individuals who have billions and billions of dollars and yet seek still more. Or, by dictators who rule over millions with the use of fear and military force and impose strict totalitarian rules over their own people. Or, by bankers and politicians who engineer wars because ultimately, they are good for business. Or, by men and women in everyday life who abuse, exploit, and manipulate those who are more vulnerable.

The tyrant believes that the security he desires can be obtained by separating himself from Nature and from all worldly responsibilities, and by having every aspect of his life controlled and mechanised. This mindset is clearly on display through what we call the "Western dream", in which the tyrant's goal is to obtain the largest mansion with the largest fence and gate blocking him off from the world. Or alternatively, the tallest penthouse suite looking down upon the world, with servants and butlers being on call for his every whim and desire, along with being chauffeured around on private jets and luxury cars, owning his own secluded island, and being treated like a VIP wherever he goes. This Western dream is lauded as the highest level of success in our tyrant-controlled culture, even if we have to sacrifice all of our health, happiness, and relationships to obtain it.

In contrast, the inner female does not seek security through power, control, material possessions, and by striving for immortality. Instead, she deeply desires to be in relationship with the world, surrendering herself to whatever it asks of her. She respects and honours harmony, Wholeness, and freedom above all else, and she does not see herself as above or below anything in this world. For she understands that everything from microscopic life, insects, and plants, to animals, birds, and humans are simply unique expressions of the one Great Spirit. She senses and directly feels the intelligence and force of this Great Spirit permeating through and harmonising the Universe, and she wishes to join in with this harmony rather than control it. Therefore, she is always asking, "How can I give back and serve the Great Spirit?" The tyrant, on the other hand, is always asking, "How can I take to serve my needs?"

The inner female is wild and untameable and despises conformity and perfectionism, preferring things raw and as they are without any masks. She represents the wild animal within us, the part that desires to roam free and be pulled by excitement, passion, and joy. Her honouring of freedom for herself and all lifeforms means that she does not wish to place animals in a cage, or to use them for entertainment and as accessories. Neither does she wish to control and exploit other humans to serve her own needs, nor would she ever interfere with someone else's unique spiritual development.

She allows nothing external to impose its will over her, as the only authority she surrenders to is Spirit, and she grants this same freedom to all others. This level of freedom is exceptionally fear-inducing and threatening to the tyrant, for it is the polar opposite to how he perceives the world, and if allowed to flourish it would mean the end of his existence. This is why the tyrants of the Cult impose never-ending surveillance, strict laws and regulations, fear-based propaganda, insidious mind programming techniques, and spiritual suppression. For they see the female element of humanity as their mortal enemy and as something to be controlled and crushed, but this just represents how deeply they fear her for she is the only thing that can conquer them.

CHAPTER 7

THREE KEY STAGES OF SPIRITUAL AWAKENING

1: THE INNER LONGING

The spiritual awakening process generally begins with a sense of longing that rises from deep within and calls to us like a faint whisper. Whilst it starts off faint, it gradually grows stronger and much more difficult to ignore. This longing is the voice of Spirit, beckoning the ego personality, which we are identified with, back into union with its will. The problem is that when most of us first receive this faint whisper from Spirit, we are disembodied and stuck up in the head and therefore it does not successfully capture our attention. Or, if it does, we either ignore it or mistake it for something else, as we are attempting to interpret it through the programmed and distorted lens of the ego personality. For example, we may interpret it to be a longing to obtain more ego-based desires that the Cult has programmed into our mind. Such as obtaining more money and popularity, a different shaped body, a new job, or a new relationship, just to name a few. The problem is that by solely pursuing and identifying with these types of goals and desires, we become more deeply entrenched within the will of the ego personality, and we move further away from Spirit.

Spirit, however, patiently awaits its chance to capture our attention once again, and its opportunity normally arises in times when we are experiencing intense emotional states such as sadness, grief, and depression, or when we become either sick or burned out. This is because it is only in these states that our identification with and attachment to the ego personality tends to soften. We also tend to take a pause and go into solitude and self-reflection, which provides us with a short reprieve from the endless distractions of the external world. As a result, little cracks in the emotional armour our ego personality has developed begin to appear, and through these cracks the longing voice of Spirit again begins to call.

Ideally, this time we have learned from our past mistakes of solely chasing ego-based desires, and instead interpret the longing voice of Spirit more accurately. If this is the case, we may then feel inspired to begin pursuing goals of a deeper and more spiritual nature. These may include embarking on Spiritual embodiment, healing old wounds and relationships, exploring traditional shamanic healing modalities, improving our health and fitness, moving into a career that is more exciting and nurturing for our soul, and researching esoteric and spiritual knowledge.

Although, if we again misinterpret the longing call from Spirit, it does not mean that we have failed. It just means our attachment to the ego personality is still too strong for Spirit to effectively penetrate through with enough strength and clarity. This is when Spirit will help us break down any remaining barriers by attracting into our lives powerful but often painful experiences, which may trigger deep personal suffering.

2: DISILLUSIONMENT

Our personal suffering, if powerful enough, will initiate Stage Two of *disillusionment*. Disillusionment is the process whereby our ego-based barriers that were previously blocking our connection with Spirit begin to break down. This forces us to start questioning and challenging all of the rigid values and beliefs of the ego personality that we had previously identified with, as well as causing us to question where these values and beliefs originated from. It is from this point we first begin considering the possibility that we have been deceived and lied to, which causes us to begin to scrutinise the nature of the world we've been raised in. This allows us to begin developing higher levels of discernment and critical thinking, which are important skills that will hold us in very good stead as our awakening progresses.

Disillusionment is often a painful process, for everything that is false within us begins to break down. People may even think that we are having a mental or emotional breakdown, which in a sense is true, but not in a negative sense, for what is actually breaking down is everything within us that is false. At this stage we may feel like we might not even make it out alive, and again, in a sense this is also true. For the ego personality does indeed begin to die, or at least our attachment to it begins to die, and because we have been so identified with this false part of ourselves, it feels as if we are dying with it. For this reason, many people cling to their old false illusions and beliefs and refuse to let go, but this only draws out their suffering even longer. The key in this stage is to let go and surrender to the process, no matter how painful or messy it is. For when we do this, we eventually realise that we were not truly dying, but were being reborn, and that our suffering was an initiation to higher states of being.

3: DOING THE WORK

As we progress through our disillusionment process and gradually become spiritually embodied, we find that we become filled with new insights and a vastly expanded awareness. This may sound like an entirely positive outcome, but our new awareness can also reveal things to us that we may not be ready to confront. This is because when we are identified with the ego personality, we tend to view ourselves and the world through a lens of wishful thinking and delusion. Whereas the expanded and more objective awareness of Spirit allows us to see ourselves and the world exactly as we are, with all of our light, but also all of our darkness.

This new perspective can be very sobering and confronting, as we realise the horrifying situation we find ourselves in and the immense amount of programming and manipulation that has been heaped upon us from birth. We also begin to see clearly how our entire lives have been built upon a foundation of ego-based ambitions, and the pain and destruction this has caused both to ourselves and to others. This can cause us to feel quite shocked; and to make this even more difficult is the fact that nearly everyone around us is still asleep and hypnotised. All of this must be confronted as part of the Spiritual embodiment process, as anything based upon lies and illusion will block our progress. What we also discover in this stage is that to spiritually awaken is one thing, but to form a strong and unbreakable connection with Spirit requires a huge amount of self-work. This is because absolutely everything that is blocking this connection must first be healed and removed, and for some of us the damage caused during our ego identified slumber may have been great. For example, we may awaken to find ourselves in poor health, holding many traumas, negative programming, and limiting beliefs, living solely in our heads, stuck in toxic relationships, suffering from a number of addictions, or having fallen for many of the Cult-based traps that we will confront along the way.

As a result, this stage of self-work can require many years of focused work depending on the situation we find ourselves in when we awaken, and in truth it is a lifelong process.

On the other hand, whilst this stage is defined by work, a fact that cannot be overstated, if our commitment to the work is sincere then our progress becomes unmistakable. This progress is often defined by a sense joy, peace, presence, calm, gratitude, and a deep connection to the wholeness of Nature. We become engulfed by the love of Spirit, which gradually washes away the fears and illusions of the ego personality, filling us with energy and a passion for life. Eventually, as we become more Spiritually embodied, this becomes our natural state of being.

SECTION 2

THE MATRIX CONTROL SYSTEM

CHAPTER 8

THE HIDDEN CABAL

"The conscious and intelligent manipulation of the organized habits and opinions of the masses is an important element in democratic society. Those who manipulate this unseen mechanism of society constitute an invisible government which is the true ruling power of our country. We are governed, our minds are molded, our tastes formed, our ideas suggested, largely by men we have never heard of."

~Edward Bernays, Propaganda

The true architects of the Cult operate from the shadows and exist as a secret society popularly known as the Illuminati. It is also known as the Shadow Government, the New World Order, the Babylonian Brotherhood, or the Brotherhood of the Snake. For simplicity I will refer to this secret society as the Cabal, which is defined as a secret political clique. The Cabal supposedly consists of thirteen family bloodlines, all of which are obsessed with genetic purity even to the point of interbreeding amongst each other to ensure that their genetic bloodlines do not become "polluted". These family bloodlines include the Astor, Bundy, Collins, DuPont, Freeman, Kennedy, Li, Onassis, Rockefeller, Rothschild, Russell, Van Duyne, and Merovingian bloodlines.[29] There are other associated family names within the Cabal such as the Warburgs and the Windsors; however, these families are known to change surnames in order to mask their identities, as what is most important to them is not their family name, but their bloodline genetics. The reason for this will become apparent later.

The Cabal has engineered the Cult and therefore works to ensure that everything within it runs according to its agenda, so let's do a brief recap as to how it achieves this aim. The head of the snake, so to speak, are the national and world central banks and the Fractional Reserve banking system, which allow the Cabal to control the Cult's money supply, manipulate the economy, and cripple the members of the Cult with debt. This provides the Cabal with immense power that it can then use to impose a tremendous influence over governments, manipulating them into implementing laws, regulations, and agendas that provide more power and control into the hands of the Cabal. It further uses its influence to set up the education system in a way that indoctrinates the minds of the Cult's youth whilst their perceptions of the world are still developing, and to ensure we remain spiritually disembodied. This then programs us with a Stockholm Syndrome, which causes us to develop a distorted trust and love for our captivity, whereby we defend it whenever anyone attempts to challenge it. This ensures that we remain subservient and obedient to the Cult to the very end of our lives. The Cult maintains this mind programming and hypnotised state throughout our lives by pummelling us with never-ending propaganda through the MSM. To further ensure we do not snap out of our hypnotised and programmed state when we hit adulthood, the Cabal also drains our lifeforce energy by getting us addicted to junk foods, pharmaceutical drugs, stimulants, and placing fluoride in the public water supply. This ensures that our minds are foggy and dumbed down, and that we are too exhausted to even think about resisting the Cult.

The Cabal also sets up institutions that are hierarchically designed and which require the character traits of someone who is power hungry and willing to exploit others in order to reach the very top. This has been achieved by creating a culture whereby all success within the Cult is determined by money. Therefore, if a corporation is to survive, it must generate economic profits, and the more profit it makes, the more successful it is judged to be, even if it requires exploiting others. This then creates an environment of ruthless competitiveness within the Cult, whereby those who seek to create a dominant monopoly of control in their industry are deemed as the most "successful". This ensures that those who wish to help and free humanity, and who despise exploiting others will find this environment overwhelming and will not wish to take part. These institutions have now been grown into multi-national corporations, which allows the Cabal members controlling them to make decisions that then get implemented uniformly across the world.

Through its control of the Cult's money supply, and by building dominant multi-national corporations, the Cabal now has a monopoly of control in every industry within the Cult. This includes the economy, government, the legal system, food and water, property ownership, technology, education, medicine, military, media, and religion. The Cabal's control system is far from finished, however, for its endgame agenda is complete and utter world dominance, with every country and every community on the planet under its strict control and regulation. It has achieved the first major steps of this globalisation of power already by creating global institutions that demand every nation who subscribes to these groups to acquiesce to their rules and agendas. Examples of such global institutions are the United Nations, the World Health Organisation, the International Monetary Fund, and the World Trade Organisation. The eventual goal is a one-world government, a one-world currency, a one-world bank, all protected by a world army, and all controlled by the Cabal. Within this one-world system, the entire world will be considered to be a nation, with each country to be considered as states within that nation. Although, eventually nations will be joined together, and these joined nations will be considered states, something that has already occurred with the European Union.

The Cabal selects specific members from its group to hold positions of power within the mega-institutions of the Cult, who are carefully groomed to serve the agenda of the Cabal above all else. These institution leaders serving the Cabal come together periodically through what the Cabal has called 'think tank' groups, whereby they discuss world policies. This is what the public thinks they are discussing anyway, for what they are truly discussing are plans to further the Cabal's agenda. These think tank groups include the Trilateral Commission, the Bilderberg Group, the Council on Foreign Relations, and the Club of Rome. This does not mean that everyone in these groups or every world leader understands and is privy to the Cabal's agenda, or supports it, for that matter. The Cabal is intensely secret and they uphold this secrecy by ensuring that the knowledge of their agenda is compartmentalised within a pyramid-shaped hierarchical system. This means that only those at the top of the pyramid know the true agenda of the Cabal and the exact steps of how it is to be implemented. Many of the world leaders serving the Cabal are not from the inner circle, they are simply pawns in the Cabal's game and have been manipulated or blackmailed into serving the Cabal's agenda. Or they may have been bribed or lured with the possibility of obtaining power and money. In rare cases, a genuinely altruistic and kind-hearted person who cannot be corrupted through bribes or intimidated through blackmail will somehow reach a position of power. Under such circumstances the Cabal will attempt to corrupt them and their plans through a variety of strategic attacks. Often, it will use the MSM to discredit the person's public persona, or it may even intimidate the person and their family directly. If threats do not work and the person looks like becoming a genuine threat to the Cabal's control, it will resort to assassination. Assassinations are often made to look like suicides, or alternatively, people under the influence of mind control are used to assassinate them on the Cabal's behalf, and then bear the brunt of the public backlash.[30] This ensures that the real perpetrators are protected.

Former US President John F. Kennedy (JFK) appears to have been an example of this. Like nearly every president before and after him, JFK was groomed to serve the agenda of the Cabal; however, he refused to play along as expected, and even began speaking out about the Cabal publicly, as seen in his famous 1961 speech on secret societies.

"The very word 'secrecy' is repugnant in a free and open society; and we are as a people inherently and historically opposed to secret societies, to secret oaths, and to secret proceedings.... Our way of life is under attack. Those who make themselves our enemy are advancing around the globe.... no war ever posed a greater threat to our security. If you are awaiting a finding of 'clear and present danger,' then I can only say that the danger has never been more clear and its presence has never been more imminent.... For we are opposed around the world by a monolithic and ruthless conspiracy that relies primarily on covert means for expanding its sphere of influence–on infiltration instead of invasion, on subversion instead of elections, on intimidation instead of free choice, on guerrillas by night instead of armies by day. It is a system which has conscripted vast human and material resources into the building of a tightly knit, highly efficient machine that combines military, diplomatic, intelligence, economic, scientific and political operations. Its preparations are concealed, not published. Its mistakes are buried, not headlined. Its dissenters are silenced, not praised. No expenditure is questioned, no rumour is printed, no secret is revealed."[31]

1: THE PYRAMID-SHAPED CORPORATE HIERARCHY

Let's explore how such a tiny few within the Cabal can so effectively control billions of people around the world while keeping most of the population in the dark regarding their existence. This has been achieved by constructing the basic structure of the Cult in a pyramid-shaped hierarchical fashion, whereby all knowledge, power, and control is compartmentalised and centralised to those at the very top of the pyramid. All of those on the bottom levels of the pyramid simply do what they're told and take orders from those above them, and they are only given the information they require to do their job. This is why most people within a pyramid-shaped organisation may be just good honest people who are unwittingly serving a sinister agenda without knowing it, for they are not privy to the information and agendas held by those above them. The entire Cult is set up in this pyramid shape, but it is also filled with many other smaller pyramids. What this means is that those at the very top of the pyramid, that being the Cabal, can control everyone else below, as well as keep the knowledge of their true agendas secret and compartmentalised. There is even a hierarchy that exists above the Cabal.

The Cabal view and treat the Cult's pyramid, and each nation within it, as being a part of a giant multinational corporate pyramid which they control. It appears that they run this pyramid from three main headquarters, which are the *Vatican City* in Rome, *Washington DC* in America, and the *City of London*, in London.[32] This refers not to London, the capital city of England, but to a tiny business district within London, which is technically listed as its own city, just as the tiny district of the Vatican is listed as its own city within the much larger city of Rome. Alongside these headquarters, Israel has also become a major central point where the Cabal operates in recent decades.

From these key locations within the pyramid, the Cabal can control the Cult's religion, economy, military, legal system, governments, media, and much more. The highest point of authority, or the very top of the pyramid, appears to be the Vatican in Rome. The Vatican's Catholic Church, which is ruled by Pope Francis, is one of the wealthiest and most powerful institutions on the planet and has around 1.3 billion members worldwide. World leaders from every country and religion routinely visit the Pope at Vatican City, and each time they perform ritualistic behaviours demonstrating their subservience to his authority. This includes kneeling in front of him, bowing their head, kissing his hand, and respectfully receiving instructions.[33] The British Monarchy is also a major player within the Cult's pyramid, with Queen Elizabeth II ruling over 53 countries which are collectively known as the "Commonwealth". Another major player is what is known as the House of Rothschild, which is one of the thirteen family bloodlines mentioned previously, and its control over the world's central banks is estimated to be worth many trillions of dollars.[34]

The Cabal views all of the countries of the world within its multinational corporate pyramid as subsidiary companies that it owns. It allows these countries to appear separate and independent by giving them their own names, flags, governments, and unique cultures, but in truth they are operating under the same umbrella and are all controlled within the same pyramid. This is similar to how Coca-Cola, being a major multinational corporation, also has subsidiary companies that it owns, such as Sprite, Fanta, Vitaminwater, and Powerade. Many people would drink a Vitaminwater and Powerade believing that they are their own independent companies because they have their own unique brand and style, not realising that they are all owned by Coca-Cola. This means that all the profits from these subsidiary companies flow back to Coca-Cola, and all of the major decisions about the future direction of these subsidiary companies are made by the Coca-Cola headquarters.

This multinational corporate pyramid setup is how the Cabal enforce their agenda upon the world. Each leader of every nation, as well as the leaders of the major world institutions, work for this global corporate pyramid that the Cabal owns. We could call it 'Cabal Inc.'

The analogy of the Cabal seeing the world as a major multinational corporate pyramid is more than just an analogy; it is an actual reality. In his book *UBUNTU Contributionism*, in the chapter titled "Our countries are registered as corporations", Michael Tellinger explains, "*All of this only begins to truly sink in and make sense once we see that our countries are registered as corporations. A quick search on the United States Securities & Exchange website provides the evidence. And what do listed corporations do? They trade their assets, including their citizens, on the global stock markets. But it does not stop there. The registrations of companies extend into states, provinces, cities, government departments, and even the governments themselves that are registered as corporations. The whole world around us and everything we hold dear has been turned into corporate assets, owned and controlled by some corporation somewhere—ultimately controlled by the elite banking families whose royal bloodlines go back thousands of years.*"

He then proceeds to list numerous countries around the world that are literally listed on various stock exchanges as corporations, including major Western countries such as America, Canada, and Australia.[35]

2: PRODUCTS OF THE NATIONAL CORPORATION

If our countries are listed as corporations, then what does this make us?

What this means is that we, the citizens of the corporation that is our country, are the corporation's "products", and legally, the corporation owns us. Becoming products of our national corporation begins with the signing of our birth certificate. A free and independent being is obviously not good for corporate business for it means that we are not yet a legalised product of the national corporation. However, when our birth certificate is signed by our parents, they have unwittingly certified to have us convert from a free and independent being into a 'citizen'. A citizen is something that the corporation legally owns, and the birth certificate is the legal binding document that certifies this.

Tellinger explains that, "*According to Black's Law Dictionary, the definition of a citizen is a person who pledges their allegiance to the state in exchange for benefits and privileges. Do you even know that by declaring yourself 'a citizen' you subjugate all your rights to the state (or the corporation) in exchange for a few benefits and privileges disguised as rights? Did you even bother to look up what the legal definition of a citizen actually is?*

"If our countries are corporations, it makes the people their stock and property. Our birth certificates are the stock certificates that are being traded on the stock markets. I urge you to verify all this information to feel assured of the great deception. It is time to snap out of our hypnotic state of ignorance and share this with everyone. The whole world is enslaved by those who run the corporations—the elite banking families."

As long as we agree to operate under the name given to us by our birth certificate, we are considered to be the property of the national corporation, which means that we have agreed to be controlled and dictated to by the state, and must abide by whatever rules it imposes. The word government itself points to this as it comes from the root Latin word "gubernare", which translates as "to rule".[36]

The name we are given on our official birth certificate represents what is called a "straw man", which is a person who is regarded as having no real substance or authenticity, and is basically a fictional version of ourselves created by the corporation that owns us. This is like Coca-Cola producing a new drink and giving it a new name, such as Diet Cola. In reality, it is not a Diet Cola, but a liquid concoction of chemicals, water, and gasses, but by giving it a name and some fancy labelling, this liquid concoction takes on a new identity. We too are not really our name, and we do not belong to a corporation, instead, we are simply a human being, a complex mass of organic tissue housing a Spirit, born from and belonging to Nature and nothing else. As long as we are deceived into operating under this "straw man" identity throughout our lives, the national corporation believes that it owns us. On a spiritual level, shifting from a free being to a citizen also represents the disconnection from our true self, and the identification with the illusory ego personality.

As we grow older and unknowingly adopt and identify with our corporate straw man, whenever the national corporation communicates with us through its government institution, it is always very careful to communicate only to the straw man that represents us. This is at the same time as being careful to never acknowledge the free beings that we are by birthright. Tellinger expands on this: "*Take note that the names of the corporations are written in capital letters. This is also the case on your birth certificate, driver's licence, passport, ID document and other official documents. All official correspondence we receive, displays our names in capitals, indicating that it is addressed to the corporation called MICHAEL TELLINGER. Official tombstones follow the same rules. This is not by accident, but because of what I highlighted before, regarding newborn babies becoming 'juristic persons' and 'legal fictions' the moment a birth certificate is signed. The government and all their corporate subsidiaries that operate under the authority of the government, see people as little corporations or legal fictions, or juristic persons or even natural persons, and specifically property, under the control and the authority of the government.*

"*This notion is highlighted in the British Cestui Que Vie Act of 1666. The Act describes the set-up of a trust where people who are lost at sea would have to prove that they are not dead within seven years. However, it includes the notion that it's not just for those people who are lost at sea, but for all people. Therefore, all people are declared legally dead until proven otherwise. This is why the system believes we are dead, and does not 'see' living people, it only sees administrators (trustees) of a trust. And any administrator (trustee) who receives benefits from a trust, must pay a fee or tax for using such a benefit. This is why we pay taxes, etc. because our 'income' does not come to us, it comes into the trust which we are administering. That trust is our name in capital letters, represented by a special certificate—our birth certificate.*

"*A good example of this can be seen in the movie* Castaway, *where Tom Hanks plays a guy who is stranded on an island for 5 years. After being rescued and returning to his home town, his friends rally around him with excitement and disbelief that he could have survived for so long on his own. In his absence, however, he was declared dead—so that the government could benefit from his estate. In a strange scene that has no real impact on the movie other than exposing our status as fictional entities, one of his friends excitedly turns to Tom saying, 'Tomorrow we bring you back to life'.*

"Clearly Tom is not dead—he is standing and conversing with his friends, and yet they have to bring his 'straw man' or 'juristic person back to life. This is so that Tom could carry on paying taxes and be controlled by the state. If he continued to walk around while being declared dead, the state would have no control over his flesh and blood human being body and could not benefit from him in any way.

"When you are asked to confirm your ID number by an official of the government or bank, you unwittingly admit that you are that special piece of paper which is marked by that ID number. You are acting on behalf of the legal fiction, representing your legal entity and not standing your ground as a living breathing human being, which is not the same thing as a piece of paper."

It is understandable if this is a bit confusing to some readers at first, for we have been lied to and deceived deeply, and therefore do not understand the nature of the system we are in. If I could summarise what has been said in as simple a form as possible, it is that we have been tricked since birth to exist and operate as legally owned products within one big fabricated game, one in which we are not seen or recognised as free independent beings. It is a game that is manipulated so that we never learn how it truly works or what the rules are, and its purpose is to enslave, control, and exploit us without us even being fully aware of it.

After we are signed over as property of the state via our birth certificate, the Cult brainwashes and shapes our minds from as young an age as possible. This is so that we become a valuable and predictable product to serve the goals and objectives of the national corporation. It is a heartless, cold, and mechanical system, which means that if millions of people need to become traumatised, abused, and conditioned in order to best suit the corporation, then that is what will occur. Those running the Cult simply view the way they treat their products (us) as being necessary actions required to implement prudent and sound business strategies.

Shaping their products to the needs of the corporation obviously cannot be successfully achieved if our parents have full control over how we are raised. Therefore, the Cult has systematically taken this control away. It has achieved this by engineering an economic environment of inflation and debt, which has forced a situation whereby in most families both parents must now invest a great deal of their time into working and building their careers to make money. This means that the child is often plonked in front of the TV or some other device from a very young age and begins bonding with the TV, absorbing all of its programming. In the past, before both parents were forced to work, at least one of the child's parents would be at home, allowing the child to bond with the parent instead. The Cult uses whatever technological device we bond with as children, such as the TV, smartphone, touchpad, and others that are similar, to program our minds with subliminal messages about how the world works and what our role within it is. Whether the messages are received through movies, shows, or advertisements, they are always the same: *"You are an obedient citizen, you love your nation, you love your government, you need us to keep you safe, we are your masters, we own you, you do not question your place."* This is when the initial spells of the Cult are cast deeply upon our young and impressionable mind. Then, before we have had a chance to develop any significant abilities to think freely or question our enslavement, we are quickly sent to school. As I elaborated in depth earlier, this is where our indoctrination into life as being controlled, owned, and dictated to by the national corporation is deeply embedded. Essentially, school is the factory that produces the Cult's products.

In our modern world, it is now considered normal that in the most important years of our development, we are bonding with technological devices and our school teachers, as much if not more than our actual parents. This means that the state can impose programming deep into our minds, using technological devices and school as the mediums to achieve this. As a result, it creates a world of "adults", who look like adults, but who still exist in a childlike mental and emotional state. A state whereby we are hopelessly dependent on our masters like a child depends upon its parents. As a result of this dependency, and the Stockholm Syndrome it creates within us, being under the control of the state is where we feel the safest. Essentially, we become domesticated into our captivity.

The desire for freedom and survival is a very strong primal drive within the human species, and therefore it is natural that a number of people will question and resent their position in the Cult. As well, many will look at the wild and free animals of Nature and wonder why they are not allowed the same freedoms. To prevent these thoughts and feelings from turning into actions of anarchy and rebellion, the Cult pummels endless propaganda into its citizens' minds. For this it mainly utilises the MSM, which as mentioned earlier, is designed not to inform, but to instil fear into our minds. It is designed to make us believe that we live in a dangerous and unsafe war-hungry world, and that the only thing that can protect us is the state and its mighty military and strict authoritarian laws. Propaganda also permeates throughout Hollywood movies, which releases an endless stream of movies glorifying war, and glorifying the protection agencies of the state like the CIA, FBI, military, and homeland security, and their high-tech military equipment. Through these movies, Hollywood is always making sure that the state and these institutions are painted as the "heroes", protecting the nation from all of the "deadly terrorists" desperately trying to attack and kill everyone. The Cult will even go as far as deliberately terrorising its own citizens via pre-engineered attacks that may kill hundreds or even thousands of innocent people, and then use media propaganda to blame the attacks on someone else. The outraged and emotionally charged public response allows the state to justify imposing harsher and more strict laws, more surveillance and tracking, and to initiate wars with other countries. All of this is done in the name of "national security", whereas in truth it is done in the name of furthering the national enslavement of its own citizens. The goal of the Cabal is complete control and enslavement of the entire world's population under one pyramid-shape corporate system. This is what we already have now, but the Cabal wishes to make this official by legally disposing of any remaining independent nations, and as mentioned previously, to then turn these nations into world states, and then world unions, all controlled by a single world government. This means that on a legal basis, all illusions of free and independent nations will be made redundant, and every citizen on the planet will be controlled and regulated directly by a world government.

John Perkins, author of *Confessions of an Economic Hit Man*, was hired by the Cabal to help absorb independent nations into this new global corporate control pyramid that they wished to create. His role was to infiltrate these countries and gain control and power over them, mainly through economic exploitation. He gives a glimpse into exactly how this extortion takes place:

"Economic hit men (EHMs) are highly paid professionals who cheat countries around the globe out of trillions of dollars. They funnel money from the World Bank, the U.S. Agency for International Development (USAID), and other foreign 'aid' organizations into the coffers of huge corporations and the pockets of a

few wealthy families who control the planet's natural resources. Their tools include fraudulent financial reports, rigged elections, payoffs, extortion, sex, and murder. They play a game as old as empire, but one that has taken on new and terrifying dimensions during this time of globalization. I should know; I was an EHM."

3: THE WORLD-WIDE THEATRICAL DRAMA

With the world's nations controlled under a single multinational corporate pyramid, the Cabal puppets we call world leaders then play their roles as actors in a massive show of theatrical drama. The Cabal decides who will be the bad guy and the hero from one week to another, as well as who will attack whom and how they will do it. In truth, apart from rare exceptions, they are all working for the same agenda, despite appearing to be enemies. Once they decide who will be the good guy and bad guy, each nation then utilises its own internal MSM to pummel the desired message into their citizens minds. They will say, *"Today Russia is your enemy"*, and another day, *"China is your enemy"*, and another day, *"South Korea is your enemy"*. Those countries will also say to their citizens, *"today America is your enemy"*, and another day, *"England is your enemy"*. The important thing is not who the enemy is, but that *there is an enemy*. For without an enemy, the endless violence, wars, military aggression, increased surveillance, deletion of human rights and personal privacy, and subsequent expansion of global power could never be justified. Therefore, just about everything that occurs between countries is simply pre-engineered theatrics designed to keep the masses in fear and servitude. If a country truly is a threat to the MCS, they are systematically crushed by the Cabal and absorbed back into the control system.

It may be difficult for some readers to comprehend that we could exist in a system based on such a massive level of lies and deception. The Cabal have been at this game for a long time and have turned controlling and deceiving humanity into a refined and systematic process. The reality is that the entire Cult that we have been indoctrinated into is based on nothing but illusion and theatre.

War itself is just a game for the Cabal, and is in fact a very reliable tool for expanding their agenda for global control. The Cabal is in such a position of power that they can finance both sides of wars, making countless billions off it no matter who wins or how many people die. G. Edward Griffin's *The Creature from Jekyll Island* documents this in methodical detail and demonstrates how deaths within wars are seen as necessary collateral damage by the Cabal. They are willing to sacrifice some of their products in order to ensure larger business gains. For, if there is a country that is demonstrating resistance to their rule and is showing signs of obtaining independence, the Cabal can use war as an excuse to invade and cripple that country into submission. They can then take control of that country's leadership and its major industries, and gradually absorb them back in line with the control system.

War cannot be justified to the public unless there is something emotionally powerful enough to justify initiating one, and the only thing powerful enough to do this is terror and fear. Therefore, to engineer this terror and fear among the public, the Cabal will stage an attack, or a series of attacks, upon its own citizens. These attacks may be in the form of a bombing, shooting, an engineered virus, or even flying planes into a set of towers. Or, there are times when a threat is actually non-existent, but by deceiving the public into believing that it is real through the MSM, it is often enough to generate the desired reaction. The purpose of these staged attacks is to get the public into such a state of terror, fear, shock, and anger that they begin demanding revenge upon the "perpetrators". The Cabal will already have pre-planned the script as to who these perpetrators are, and they will pummel that script into the minds of the public through the MSM immediately after the attacks. They will do this at the same time as continuously showing graphic and gory images of the attacks to ensure that the public experiences maximum trauma and shock. Whatever perpetrator the Cabal decides to blame these attacks on depends on which country they wish to invade and conquer. They will create a villain who is from their target country, blame the attacks upon that person, and then convince the public that they must wage war upon that person and anyone affiliated with him. It is at this point that the idea of going to war is relentlessly pushed into public's mind's through the MSM, and they achieve this by repeating simple slogans such as *"The War on Terror!"*, or, *"War is Inevitable!"*, or, *"War for Peace and National Security!"*. There will be many within the public at this point attempting to warn the masses that they are being deceived, and trying to help them see the irony and contradiction of attempting to obtain "peace through violence". Unfortunately, because the masses are blinded by fear and are deeply programmed to trust and be obedient to their masters, they disregard these people as "conspiracy theorists".

This technique has been named by researchers as the *"problem, reaction, solution"* strategy. It is named as such because when the Cabal want to move forward with an agenda, such as creating a war, they must first engineer a "problem". This is because they know full well that without a powerful catalyst, their agenda would never receive any public support. However, when there is a "threat", such as a staged terror attack, it can function as the necessary catalyst. This "problem", which as mentioned previously will be blamed upon a made-up villain, inevitably triggers a strong public "reaction", such as shock, outrage, panic, and terror. This then allows the Cabal to present their "solution". The solution always includes strategies such as increasing national security measures and surveillance, bringing in new strict terrorist laws, and waging war upon the country this "villain" came from in order to "bring them to justice". All of these "solutions" are presented in such a way that gives the appearance of increasing the safety of the public and the nation, but their true purpose is to enhance the Cabal's power and control. *Problem, reaction, solution*, is used on the public again and again with incredible success, and even though it is very predictable, it will continue to be used in the future, for why change a strategy that is so successful. Besides, even if war results, the safety of those within the Cabal is never directly threatened, for they themselves never actually go to war. They have instead sent countless millions of innocent people to their deaths on their behalf, all of whom believed that they were "serving their country". The amount of deaths caused by governments in the 20th century alone is estimated to be over 200 million[37] (I believe that is a conservative number personally), and this means that death by government is the leading cause of human deaths compared with any other cause that exists.

4: THE ILLUSION OF FREEDOM

Despite the never-ending wars, murder, corruption, control, deception, and exploitation at the hands of the Cabal, most people still falsely believe that they are free. This illusion is upheld only because by having us think that we are free, and by making us believe that our masters are "protecting us", we meekly accept the ever-strengthening controls systems that are around us without resistance. On the other hand, if as a collective we understood that we were being manipulated and enslaved, there would no doubt be an uprising and rebellion. Considering the fact that we greatly outnumber the Cabal, this is the last thing they want to happen. This is not to say that they will allow our illusion of freedom to be maintained forever, as when they are satisfied that their control systems are inescapable, the reality of our situation will become more open and obvious.

To enhance our illusion of freedom, the Cabal creates a two-party political set up allowing us to have a "choice" between which of the two Cabal-puppet leaders will rule us for the next 4-8 years. Never mind that we have no say in who these two people are, where they've come from, or why there are only two to choose from. This isn't really relevant because all that matters is that we have been deceived into believing we were given a free choice and that we live in a "democracy". The truth is that a democracy, whilst sounding good on paper, is nothing more than a charade. By creating the illusion of a democracy and of free choice where "people's votes matter", we do not notice that we are actually living under a fascist dictatorship.

Once the new leader has been "voted" into power, he always proceeds to do the exact opposite to the promises he made in his political campaign, and instead does whatever the Cabal directs him to do. As long as he gives believable enough public speeches, and the Cabal keeps the masses distracted with enough dramas and theatrics during his campaign, most do not notice. Or, if the public begins to hate and distrust him, they will project all of their frustration and anger onto him, still not realising that he is nothing more than a puppet. The true perpetrators always remain hidden in the shadows, out of reach of the public's persecutions. Whilst this leader is serving the Cabal, regular threats are engineered in order to keep the public distracted and in a constant state of fear, anxiety, and division. Such examples – some of which we touched on previously - are the threat of war, terrorist attack, economic crash, virus outbreak, extreme weather, food and water shortage, and countless other social issues.

Once this leader's 4-8 years of service to the Cabal has come to an end, a new puppet leader is presented to the masses, and the entire circus show repeats itself. This new leader will promise the same things, get "voted" into power, and then proceed to do the bidding of his masters just like the leader before him. The truth is that nearly all politicians are nothing more than professional stage men and pathological liars, placed in front of us to dazzle us with their charm, fake promises, and spellbinding words. The only thing that can bring this circus show to an end is for enough people to wake up to the illusion that it is. If a leader does somehow sneak through the cracks and attempt to actually serve the people, they are seen as threats to the agenda of the Cabal and are dealt with accordingly.

This is of course not to say there are never any authentic threats or deliberate outside attacks upon a country, but even many of these are either directly or indirectly provoked by the actions of the Cabal. John Perkins explains that, "*The* (Cabal controlled; Author's note) *United States spends over $87 billion conducting a war in Iraq while the United Nations estimates that for less than half that amount, we could provide clean water, adequate diets, sanitation services and basic education to every person on the planet. And we wonder why terrorists attack us.*"

Another key tactic the Cabal uses to distract and divide us is to engineer public debates around emotionally charged topics that are typically deemed by us as being important issues. The main tool used here is again the MSM, which generates divisive headlines and stories, which then spread throughout the social media networks like wildfire. From our perspective it appears that an important social issue has just "appeared out of nowhere", but this couldn't be further from the truth. The goal here is to engineer a debate around a topic that is divisive by its very nature, and which leads to arguing and fighting among people. The Cabal then deliberately provokes both sides of the issue in order to create a more intense level of division, conflict, and fighting. The purpose of this is so that we become even more divided, ensuring that our chances of unifying and rebelling against the Cabal are minimal. This is the age-old technique of divide and conquer, and what works best for this tactic are emotionally triggering topics such as vaccinations, climate change, racial and gender equality, immigration, birth control, gun laws, diet, and many other issues.

The divide-and-conquer tactics used most commonly against us are Machiavellian by nature. This is a term used to describe anyone in politics or in a position of authority who maintains and expands their power through the use of cunning, devious, and treacherous tactics. One of the most well-known Machiavellian tactics, which has been used time and again throughout history and is used on us frequently today, is to deliberately stir up friction and conflict by telling lies to both parties. The real perpetrator then steps back and allows these two parties to fight it out, whilst they pretend to be the benevolent third party who steps in with force in order to maintain "peace and order".

In his book *Gods of Eden*, William Bramley elaborates on the Machiavellian tactics and how they came about: *"One of the most famous philosophers to discuss third-party manipulation as a tool of social and political control was Niccolo Machiavelli, the sixteenth-century philosopher. Although Machiavelli was not the first to write about these matters, his name has become synonymous with unscrupulous political cunning.*

"Machiavelli authored several unsolicited 'how-to' manuals for the benefit of a local prince. Those writings have become literary classics. In them, Machiavelli describes several of the techniques used by various Italian rulers to maintain control over a population. One method was to breed conflict.

"In his treatise, The Prince, *Machiavelli wrote: 'Some princes, so as to hold securely the state, have disarmed their subjects, others have kept their subject towns distracted by factions (disputes)…'*

"Machiavelli cites a specific example: 'Our forefathers, and those who were reckoned wise, were accustomed to say that is was necessary to hold Pistoia (an Italian city) by factions and Pisa by fortress, and with this idea they fostered quarrels in some of their tributary towns so as to keep possession of them more easily.'

"Human disunity was a valuable commodity to the princes because it made the people less able to mount a challenge. Machiavelli described the exact steps to be taken by anyone wishing to employ this tool: 'The way to set about this is to win the confidence of the city which is disunited; and, so long as they do not come to blows, to act as arbitrator between the parties, and, when they come to blows, to give the tardy support to the weaker party, both with a view to keeping them at it and wearing them out; and, again because stronger measures would leave no room for any doubt that you were out to subjugate them and make yourself their ruler. When this scheme is carried out, it will happen, as always, that the end you have in view will be attained. The city of Pistoia, as I have said in another discourse and apropos of another topic, was acquired by the republic of Florence by just such an artifice; for it was divided and the Florentines supported now one, now the other party and, without making themselves obnoxious to either, led them on until they got sick of their turbulent way of living and then in the end came to throw themselves voluntarily into the arms of Florence.'

"This phenomenon can be observed on a personal level when two friends discover that a third 'friend' has been saying derogatory things about each one to the other behind their backs. For the technique to be effective, the perpetrator must remain hidden from view as the source of the conflict.

"To summarize the observations of Machiavelli, we find that breeding conflict between people can be an effective tool for maintaining social and political control over a populace. For the technique to be effective, the instigator must do the following:

1. *Erect conflicts and 'issues' which will cause people to fight amongst themselves rather than against the perpetrator.*

2. *Remain hidden from view as the true instigator of the conflicts.*

3. *Lend support to all warring parties.*

4. *Be viewed as the benevolent source which can solve the conflicts."*

Anyone free from the programming of the Cult will be able to clearly see that these same Machiavellian tactics are being used on us today with incredible success. They are even more successful today because the modern Cabal have technologies that the Cabal in Machiavelli's day (1469-1527) did not possess. With these technologies, they now have access to our minds every single day, something that those in the days of Niccolo Machiavelli would have clearly relished.

CHAPTER 9

THE PSYCHOPATHIC NATURE OF THE CABAL

The idea that humanity is living within a systematic, meticulously planned, ruthless, and downright evil Cult is overwhelming and unimaginable to most people, and this is why the common response to this information is that of rejection, ridicule, and disbelief. As mentioned previously, this reflex trigger reaction is the result of cognitive dissonance created by a lifetime of Cult programming. However, one other reason people tend to reflexively reject this information without further consideration or research is because they project their own inner nature onto the Cabal and their puppet world leaders. When confronted with the sort of information revealed in this book, people may say, *"no one would ever do something like that, that's ridiculous!"* What they mean here is that "they", or at least the average person, would never do anything like that, which is because most people desire peace and are kind-hearted and empathic at their deepest nature. Whilst this is true for the average person, it is certainly not true for a particular breed of person.

The field of psychopathy, a branch of psychology that studies psychopaths, has well established over many decades of meticulous research that around 4-6% of the population are genetic psychopaths. The term "psycho" relates to the mind and soul, and 'path' relates to having a disease, meaning that a psychopath suffers from a "disease of the mind and soul".

A psychopath is internally wired differently than other people, and subsequently cannot experience normal human emotions such as love and empathy. The consequence of this is that they have nothing within them that could provide a direct link to Spirit, meaning that they are essentially spiritually empty. Psychopaths feed off and gain pleasure from generating pain and suffering, just as a normal person gains pleasure from generating love and happiness. They are never going to change, and they will never see the world from the empathy-oriented perspective of the average person.

In essence, they are pure predators, especially gifted at the art of deception, manipulation, and mimicry. By mimicry, I refer to how they expertly mimic the traits of a non-psychopathic person in order to avoid detection. They can even come across as incredibly charming, noble, thoughtful, altruistic, sane, and charismatic. This allows them to disarm their victims, encourage them to be vulnerable and open up about their fears, and then skilfully and meticulously exploit those fears and control them in every way possible. Once they are finished with one person and can exploit them no longer, they will simply move onto the next victim without an ounce of conscience or guilt.

Psychopaths are also wired in a way whereby they have zero fear of authority, of being punished, or of being judged by others; therefore, no amount of threats or laws will stop them doing what they desire to do. They are purely cold, calculating and emotionless predators, and they see themselves like a cat in a world of mice.[38] Many of the Cabal-controlled world leaders that are paraded in front of us, and who dazzle us with their charm and smooth words, are genetic psychopaths.

It has been well established through research that psychopaths excel at climbing up corporate ladders and entrenching themselves in positions of power. This is because their skilful mimicking abilities allow them to present themselves in a way that is well liked and approved by their superiors. They have at the same time an underlying terrifying ruthlessness and lack of conscience that allows them to go to extreme lengths in order to succeed. This gives them a distinct competitive advantage because they are willing to do things that a normal person would never do, and they have no hesitation in capitalising on this advantage. This includes things such as exploiting another person's fears in order to erode their self-confidence, or exploiting another person's trust and kindness.

Dr. Robert Hare, author of *Without Conscience*, explains that, "*Too many people hold the idea that psychopaths are essentially killers or convicts. The general public hasn't been educated to see beyond the social stereotypes to understand that psychopaths can be entrepreneurs, politicians, CEOs and other successful individuals who may never see the inside of a prison. Psychopaths have what it takes to defraud and bilk others: They are fast-talking, charming, self-assured, at ease in social situations, cool under pressure, unfazed by the possibility of being found out, and totally ruthless. The psychopath can actually put themselves inside your skin intellectually, not emotionally. They can tell what you're thinking, in a sense, they can look at your body language, they listen to what you're saying, but what they don't really do is feel what you feel. What this allows them to do is to use the words to manipulate and con and interact with you, without the baggage of this 'I really feel your pain'."*

Researching the nature of psychopaths helps us to understand why we cannot attempt to discern the Cabal and their agenda by projecting our own empathic nature onto them. We are dealing with predators and masters of deception who seek only to control and exploit others for their own benefit and pleasure. The sooner we can come to terms with this reality, the sooner we can learn to both understand this predator and to defend ourselves against them.

CHAPTER 10

THE OCCULT FORCES BEHIND THE CABAL

A distinguishing feature of the Cabal is how well organised they are, and how effectively their agenda for complete global control is implemented with ruthless, systematic, and patient progression, even over multiple generations. This slow and methodical progression is how an author like George Orwell was able to write his book *1984*, all the way back in 1949, which accurately predicted much of the world we see around us today, including technologies that were not yet invented in his time. Similarly, Aldous Huxley wrote his prophetic dystopian novel *Brave New World* back in 1932, which also accurately predicted many of the specific control mechanisms that we see in our world today. This is because both authors, along with their obvious intelligence and writing talent, supposedly had a certain level of access to the inside information of the Cabal's agenda. Therefore, they knew what was coming and were attempting to warn us.

The thing that makes this long-term systematic organisation of the Cabal's agenda so mind-boggling is that decades of research into psychopathy has revealed that psychopaths typically do not work well in teams or groups and are known to be highly erratic, impulsive, and unpredictable. This is even to the point whereby they themselves are not always entirely sure what they will do next. How then, is the Cabal so well organised and unified in their objectives? Are they a different type of psychopath than the ones studied in the general public? It is my opinion that the Cabal stay so well organised because they themselves are not on top of the control pyramid hierarchy, and are being controlled and organised by hidden negative forces that are not of human origins.

All true esoteric schools of thought have spoken about both positive and negative hidden forces and their influences over humanity. In truth, all life is under the influence of hidden forces, which is something that those who have become spiritually embodied can begin to perceive directly. This means that despite our illusions of free will, and of being in control of our thoughts and actions, we are instead being pulled to and fro by forces that lie beyond the veil of our ordinary awareness. This is particularly the case for negative hidden forces, who are much more willing and eager to impose on and manipulate lower density beings like us, than are positive higher forces.

Referring to how these hidden forces influence humanity, Indian mystic and philosopher Sri Aurobindo writes, *"Looking at what happened in 1914* (WW1; Author's note)*—or for that matter at all that is and has been happening in human history—the eye of the Yogin* (spiritually embodied seeker; Author's note) *sees not only the outward events and persons and causes, but the enormous forces which precipitate them into action. If the men who fought were instruments in the hands of rulers and financiers, these in turn were mere puppets in the clutch of those hidden forces. When one is habituated to see the things behind, one is no longer prone to be touched by the outward aspects—or to expect any remedy from political, institutional or social changes; the only way out is through the descent of a consciousness which is not the puppet of these forces but is greater than they are."*

Whilst this may seem like an out-there topic for some and akin to science fiction, the idea of hidden forces influencing and manipulating humanity is far from a new concept. In fact, nearly every esoteric and mystic tradition has warned about negative forces. In Christianity, they are known as Demons or the devil; in Native American traditions they are known as Wetiko; in Sufism as the Shaitans; in Gnosticism as the Archons; in Hermeticism as the Lords of Destiny; in Islamic traditions as the Jinn; in Hinduism as the Asuras; in Caribbean tribal cultures as the Jumbee; in Australian Indigenous cultures as the Mamu; in Jewish Kabballah as Shedim; and in Carlos Castaneda's famous book *The Active Side of Infinity*, he refers to these negative forces as the Predator/Fliers and describes this topic as the "topic of all topics".

However, one of the biggest fields of study into hidden forces has been the UFO phenomenon. The UFO phenomenon has been occurring for a very long time, with sightings and paranormal activity even being reported thousands of years ago, but has increased in activity significantly over the last 70-100 years. In that time, serious researchers, including doctors, scientists, and investigative journalists, have dedicated their lives to getting to the bottom of the many mysteries it has presented. Some even began their research with the intention of debunking the phenomenon only to realise that something very real was occurring, and others were forced into researching it reluctantly as a result of being the victims of invasive abductions. The Cabal have attempted to do everything in their power to keep the UFO phenomenon secret and hidden, and to discredit and ridicule it so that very few take it seriously. But the reality remains that many thousands of people all around the world have been impacted by this phenomenon with experiences ranging from spooky and unexplainable paranormal activity to abductions that involve invasive surgeries and even rape and torture. If the reader wishes to pursue deeper research into this phenomenon and the many case studies it has presented, I highly recommend the works of Karla Turner, John Keel, Jacques Vallée, Richard Dolan, Bernhard Guenther, and Tom Montalk.

Whilst there is still a great deal of mystery surrounding this phenomenon, one thing that has become clear is that the beings involved are very hostile to humanity. In addition, they are masters at deception, often depicting themselves as positive and even angelic beings. This is something that Dr. Karla Turner exposed at length in her 1994 book *Masquerade of Angels*. What has become apparent to researchers who have looked deeply into this phenomenon is that humanity is being heavily exploited and even farmed by these beings, which I will now refer to as the NHF's (negative hostile forces). In his book *The Active Side of Infinity*, Carlos Castaneda reveals this information in his discussions with Yaqui sorcerer Don Juan Matus. Don Juan explains, *"You have arrived, by your effort alone, to what the shamans of ancient Mexico called the topic of topics. I have been beating around the bush all this time, insinuating to you that something is holding us prisoner. Indeed, we are held prisoner! This was an energetic fact for the sorcerers of ancient Mexico."*

"Why has this predator taken over in the fashion that you're describing, Don Juan?" I asked. "There must be a logical explanation."

"There is an explanation", Don Juan replied, "which is the simplest explanation in the world. They took over because we are food for them, and they squeeze us mercilessly because we are their sustenance. Just as we rear chickens in chicken coops, the predators rear us in human coops. Therefore, their food is always available to them."

The food that we provide these beings that Castaneda was referring to is our very essence, our lifeforce energy. The reason these predators must feed off the lifeforce energy of other beings is because they have chosen to pursue the path of evil and service to self, meaning that they have cut themselves off from the life-giving energies of the Great Spirit. And for the lifeforce energy of other beings, such as humans, to be nourishing for them, it must first be corrupted and distorted in order to match their vibrational frequency. Positive emotional states such as love must first be converted to hate, confidence into anxiety, trust into fear, calmness into terror, and so on.

Tom Montalk explains that, *"What we call 'aliens' are hyperdimensional* (higher density; Author's note) *beings. They hide behind the veil of our perceptions and can project themselves into our visible reality at will. They are not recent visitors to earth, but have been here for hundreds of thousands of years and continue to live here, mostly in underground bases. Some 'aliens' helped genetically engineer the human race, while other factions later crippled human genetics in order to turn mankind into little more than a source of physical and etheric food. Literature tends to identify these negative 'aliens' as the reptilians, grays, mantids, and some hostile nordic factions. There exist positively oriented beings as well, notably the more positive nordics, but they respect the law of freewill and do not engage in physical abductions. Rather they exist as a spiritual brotherhood lending their service to protect and guide those of us who seek freedom from the limitations of this 3D matrix control system, prison/school earth."*[39]

If the Cult is ultimately engineered and controlled by hostile beings from higher densities, then that would explain why the Cabal do what they do and how they are so well organised. Don Juan again explains, *"What I'm saying is that what we have against us is not a simple predator. It is very smart, and organized. It follows a methodical system to render us useless."*

It appears that the psychopathic Cabal are a genetically altered faction of the human race, engineered to be used as puppets for the NHF's, with the task of controlling and farming humanity on behalf of their masters. This also further explains why the Cabal is so obsessed with interbreeding and maintaining genetic purity, for the NHF's do not want their psychopathic genetics to become diluted.

CHAPTER 11

HUMANITY'S MYSTERIOUS ORIGINS

The idea that we are a slave race serving another worldly or dimensional force is not new by any means. Ancient Sumerian tablets (and keep in mind that Sumer was an advanced civilisation with a flourishing and sophisticated culture) depict a very unusual tale of human creation. They speak of a race of "God-like" aliens with a human-like appearance, who came to Earth hundreds of thousands of years ago in order to mine Earth for her precious minerals. Supposedly these beings found the effort required to achieve this on our dense planet quite difficult. One tablet says, *"When the Gods like men, bore the work and suffered the toil, the toil of the Gods was great. The work was heavy, the distress was much."*

As a result, the tablets explain how these beings supposedly created the modern human, in a story that sounds like they are describing biological engineering much in the same way we might attempt to genetically engineer a specific type of animal species today. The newly created species was then designated the role of a slave race to its God-like masters and were subsequently treated brutally. Many other indigenous cultures around the world also tell stories and myths that point to other-worldly beings interfering with the human race.

How does this Sumerian story fit in with what modern science has discovered about the human timeline and our genetics?

We are told that humans came about as a result of millions and millions of years of slow Darwinian-style evolution, and that we gradually evolved from simple cells to more complex animals, and eventually to primates and then humans.

This, however, directly conflicts with what modern science has discovered about human origins in recent years. When scientists began mapping the human genome a number of decades ago, which is our genetic DNA, they expected to once and for all solve the riddle about how modern humans came about. They also expected to find the "missing link" that would prove modern humans evolved from primates, a missing link that has never been found in the fossil record.

What they found by studying human genetics and comparing them with other animals only created more questions and mystery. It turns out humans did not evolve slowly on this planet, but rather appeared suddenly many millennia ago. In his book *The Science of Self-Empowerment*, scientist Gregg Braden explains that, *"Fact 1: The relationships shown on the conventional human evolutionary tree—the dashed lines that connect one fossil to another and lead to modern humans at the top of the tree—are not based on evidence. While these relationships are believed to exist, they have never been proven and are inferred or speculative relationships.*

"Fact 2: Modern humans arose suddenly on earth approximately 200,000 years ago with the advanced features that set us apart from all other known forms of life already developed.

"Fact 3: The lack of common DNA between ancient Neanderthals, thought to be some of our ancestors, and early humans, whose DNA is similar to ours, tells us that we did not originally descend from the Neanderthals, even if we interbred with them at some point.

"Fact 4: Advanced genome analysis reveals that the DNA that sets us apart from other primates is the result of an ancient, mysterious, and precise fusion of genes that suggests something beyond evolution made our humanness possible.

"To be clear, the advanced features identified in Fact 2 didn't develop slowly over long periods of time, as evolutionary theory would suggest. Instead, characteristics that include a brain 50 percent larger than that of our nearest primate relative and a complex nervous system with emotional and sensory abilities fine-tuned to our world already existed in modern humans when they appeared. And humans haven't changed. In other words, contemporary humans are the same humans, 2,000 centuries later!"

Despite the mystery surrounding our origins, we do share a large amount of DNA with other lifeforms on this planet, and it is by studying these similarities that we begin to find clues about what makes us so different. Through genome mapping, it was found that humans share a massive 98.5%

DNA with chimpanzees, but what was even more remarkable was how much DNA we shared with non-primates. For example, Gregg Braden explains that *"we share 60 percent of our DNA with a fruit fly, 80 percent with a cow, and 90 percent with a common house cat"*.

This raises the question: if we modern humans share so much DNA with a chimp, and even share a great deal of DNA with other animals such as cats, cows, and insects such as the fruit fly, why then are we so remarkably different? What made things even more confusing was that it was discovered that whilst a chimp's DNA contains 48 chromosomes, human DNA contains only 46 chromosomes. So why are we missing chromosomes, where did they go, and why are we more advanced despite having fewer chromosomes?

It turns out that these things can occur because different genes can be activated and thus express themselves in a variety of different ways, depending on how they are coded. As human DNA sequencing continued, it was discovered that our missing chimp DNA had somehow mutated and morphed together into larger chromosomes, and these larger chromosomes were hiding the missing smaller ones.

Braden explains, *"It appears that long ago two separate chromosomes from chimpanzees (chimp chromosomes 2A and 2B) merged or fused into the single, larger human chromosome 2—which is one of the key chromosomes that give us our humanness. Many of the characteristics that make us uniquely human arise from the DNA fusion that resulted in human chromosome 2. HC2* (human chromosome 2; Author's note)*-linked traits include qualities such as our intellect, the growth and development of our brains in general, and specifically the largest part of our brain, the cortex, which is associated with the way we think and act and our capacity for emotion."*

This mutation is remarkable in itself, and seems to explain why humans are so unique and why our intellects are so advanced compared to all other animal species, but as Braden explains, it becomes even more interesting: *"It's the way these smaller chromosomes combined that may solve the mystery of mutations such as those in FOXP2* (a protein found in humans that also went through remarkable and unexplainable mutations, giving us our unique ability to talk, Authors note), *and ultimately, the mystery of human origins. While scientists acknowledge that the mutations definitely occurred in FOXP2 and that they happened within the time frame that correlates with the rise of anatomically modern humans, they can't really tell us what caused the change. But they can tell with chromosome 2. And it's this difference that sets chromosome 2 apart.*

"…human chromosome 2 has preserved a record of how it came to exist. It's what this forensic evidence may truly reveal to us that has opened the door to so much speculation. This is where the story of our past takes an unexpected turn, with deeper implications that make our origins begin to sound like the theme of a really good science-fiction novel.

"You see, the Proceedings of the National Academy of Sciences study states that although this kind of fusion is known to happen occasionally, it's rare. What accompanied the fusion itself opens the door to our new human story. In the language of the researchers describing this discovery, the fusion was either "accompanied or followed by inactivation or elimination of one of the ancestral centromeres, as well as by events which stabilize the fusion point." While this language is admittedly complex, the message is clear and simple. The study is telling us that during the fusion, or immediately afterward, the overlapping functions from what were originally two separate chromosomes were either adjusted, turned off, or removed altogether to make the new single chromosome more efficient. This fact strongly implies intentionality. And as we've discovered previously, that intentionality led to humanity's possession of many of the extraordinary functions that are found in no other form of life on earth. Two questions: Why and how?"

The key thing that Braden mentions here is that the way the Chromosome 2 fused *"strongly implies intentionality"*, as this supports the Sumerian story that humans were genetically created and engineered by advanced beings. These beings potentially had technology that allowed them to perform DNA mixing, splicing, and modifications, much like we can do today. Sumerian tablets state that the first human was born inside the womb of one of the female God-like beings, by mixing the blood of one of their fellow gods that they killed with the clay of the Earth. This implies that they genetically mixed their own DNA with DNA from something on Earth, and then grew the first human inside one of their females. This may sound completely implausible to some; however, our modern science is currently on the brink of being able to grow human organs inside of other animals in order to use them for transplants.[40] We are also beginning to grow baby lambs within artificial wombs.[41] If this is what we can do now, think of what we will be able to do in fifty to one hundred years, or even in just five to ten years.

Another thing to consider is that human DNA supposedly contains what has been called "junk DNA". If there is indeed junk DNA within the human genome that can't be assigned any functions, could it be that this was switched off deliberately? Nature does not do "junk" anything, for everything that is created serves a function; therefore, if something within us doesn't function, it may be a sign that it has been tampered with. This would certainly suit our creators who wished to enslave us, especially if they managed to switch off certain psychic or intuitive centres that would otherwise have given us a more expanded awareness and intelligence. And, if this is the case, can we possibly re-activate this switched-off DNA?

This alternative theory of human origins certainly would explain why humans are so unique. Very few people stop to really think about how different we are from all of the other species on this planet, and how alien our features, such as the ability to talk, think abstractly, and build complex civilisations, really are. We are told that it is the result of slow evolution, but the scientific evidence ranging from the findings in the genome project to the lack of fossil evidence suggests a different story. The evidence is telling us that we appeared suddenly, with all of our advanced traits already intact. Slow Darwinian evolution certainly does not work that way, as it would potentially require tens of millions of years to develop the advanced traits we display. On top of this, the likelihood that the complex and specific mutations that occurred in our Chromosome 2 and FOXP2 protein could have happened by random chance are very low. Could we have been engineered the way we are so that we could be a highly efficient slave race? A slave race intelligent enough to take care of ourselves and reproduce without requiring constant care from our masters, but not intelligent or advanced enough to be a genuine threat. This is not a farfetched concept, for we humans even do this to other animals already, whereby we genetically breed animal species in order to suit our purposes, and then we enslave and exploit them. We see nothing wrong with this, of course, for we are simply doing what we need to do to eat and survive, but this is most likely no different to the mindset of the beings farming us, for they too require food. It just means that we must come to terms with the horrifying reality that we may not be on top of the food chain like we thought ourselves to be.

Although, is it possible that these beings above us on the food chain engineered us with too much intelligence and have underestimated how advanced we are? This could explain why they need to go to such great lengths to program us into the Cult in order keep us under their control.

CHAPTER 12

THE NATURE OF REALITY AND HUMAN FARMING

How is it possible that beings could be not only exploiting us but also systematically farming us for our lifeforce energy without us being aware of it? In order to discuss how this is possible, it is important to understand how limited our perception of reality really is, and how much more limited it has become as a result of genetic engineering and our programming within the Cult.

What we call reality is what we experience through the body and its five senses of sight, sound, touch, taste, and smell. These senses allow us to decode a certain bandwidth of light from what is known as the Electromagnetic Frequency (EMF) light spectrum into what we experience as a tangible reality. The EMF light spectrum is a field of energy that contains light which vibrates at different speeds, and these vibrations are measured in terms of the frequency at which they vibrate per second, which is why they are referred to as "frequencies" or "vibrations". Our senses receive these vibrations in their energetic form, and then through a mind-boggling process of chemical reactions, converts them into what we can see, touch, taste, hear, and feel around us. Essentially, without the body and its senses, what we call reality simply would not exist.

The EMF spectrum is broken up into different segments which are determined by their rate of vibrating frequencies, and these include radio waves, microwaves, infrared, ultraviolet, X-ray, and gamma rays. Radio wave frequencies vibrate the slowest within this spectrum, and gamma rays vibrate the fastest; however, there are also different rates of frequencies within each segment. The light within the EMF spectrum consists of non-physical energy and therefore has no tangible form, that is, until something decodes the information that this light carries into a tangible reality. The human body is such a technology, and it is what our Spirit utilises in order to experience a small section of this spectrum in a way that it otherwise could never experience. However, when I say small, I mean small, for it is estimated that we can only decode around 0.35% of the entire EMF spectrum, which is the part that we call "visible light". This means that there are vast levels of reality that exist all around us in their energetic form, but we cannot perceive them. The human body also creates the illusion of physicality, whereas in truth no physicality can truly exist for everything is energy at its base form. The body also creates the illusion of what we know of as linear time, whereby there is a past, present, and future, but again, outside of the body time does not exist.

What all this is pointing to is that what we experience on a day-to-day basis that we believe is "reality" is an incredibly tiny and illusory aspect of reality, and there is much more that exists around us that we cannot decode. It is only by understanding this that we can comprehend how higher density beings can exist within the same space as we do, and yet operate beyond our sensory awareness. This occurs because these beings inhabit segments of the EMF light spectrum that our limited senses cannot decode. This is similar in concept to how an ant may be crawling across our skin, and yet have no comprehension that it is on another living being. This is because it only has a limited range of senses designed mostly to find food for its colony; it cannot fully decode our existence. Nature creates various lifeforms with varying degrees of reality decoding abilities, and whilst we are quite advanced in terms of what we can decode and understand compared to other lifeforms, we are also extremely limited.

The idea that multiple realities, or fields of information, can exist overlapping each other in the same space can also be difficult to grasp, but this occurs because they utilise different frequencies within that space. Researcher David Icke uses the analogy of a radio broadcasting station to explain how this works: a central radio station broadcasts on different radio wave frequencies, or "radio stations", all of which carry different information. One radio station may broadcast pop music, one jazz music, and another rock music. These radio stations share the same space within the air and therefore overlap each other; but again this is possible because they are operating on slightly different frequencies. Radio station frequencies are measured in millions of vibrations per second, with one million vibrations per second commonly shown as 1 MHz. Therefore, the pop music station may be broadcast out at 100.3MHz, the jazz station at 101.9MHz, and the rock station at 105.1MHz. Using the technology we call a radio, we can then decide which of these frequencies to tune in to. If we change our mind and switch frequencies on the radio, we call this "changing the channel". Before the radio was invented, the idea that EMF light energy waves could be used to broadcast musical information out into the air over thousands of kilometres, and then be listened to through a machine, would have sounded ludicrous.

The EMF light decoding technology known as the human body is analogous to a radio, as it allows us—Spirit—to tune in to a tiny range of these frequencies known as visible light, whereas higher density beings can tune in to a more expanded range of "channels" within the EMF light spectrum. These higher density beings also do not experience physicality and time in the same way. Instead, they exist either in a semi-physical or completely non-physical state, and appear to have the ability to travel backward or forward in what we call the past, present, and future. When these beings use their technology or abilities to access our lower frequencies, they are "changing the channel" of their reality, and when we witness them doing this, we call this paranormal or UFO activity. Unfortunately, just as there are predators within our reality, there are also predators within higher realities, and yet because they are non-physical predators, they seek non-physical food. Our lifeforce energy is to them a highly valuable source of food. But because these predators are mostly non-physical, they find it difficult to remain in our density for too long, and this is why they have genetically engineered those within the Cabal to operate their human farming operation for them.

Why do these beings work so diligently to ensure that we do not notice their influence over our lives from beyond our veil of perception? The answer to this lies in understanding that the loosh that we produce for them as food must be genuine and authentic, otherwise it is not nutritious food for them. Therefore, for authentic negative emotional loosh such as fear, terror, depression, and anxiety to be extracted, we must first be programmed to believe that we are free. This is because it is only by sincerely believing ourselves to be free can we then be filled with genuine terror at the prospect of having that freedom taken away at any moment. A being that knows it is enslaved, on the other hand, becomes accustomed to being enslaved, falls into apathy, and therefore no longer produces much if any energy. The fact that the negative loosh we produce must be authentic provides a major strategic advantage for us over the NHF's, one that if utilised on a large enough scale could implode this global human farming operation from within.

To give us the illusory perception of freedom, the NHF's utilise methods similar to what we use in our practise of "free-range" animal farming, a method of farming that allows animals to roam unrestrained, rather than being locked permanently in a confined space. This serves the purpose of meeting basic ethical standards, but also, free-range animals are thought to produce higher quality products. For example, a farmer wanting to use a cow for meat would know full well that keeping it imprisoned would have negative consequences. This is because, in captivity, animals get stressed and produce cortisol from fear, not to mention the lack of proper sunshine, fresh air, and exercise. The cow's products would therefore become less nutritious to the consumer. If, instead, the cow is given the "freedom" to roam around a pasture of green grass, exercising out in the sunshine, breathing fresh air, and socialising with the other steers and cows, it would produce higher quality products.

The catch is, whilst the cow is given the perception of freedom, it does not have true freedom. Humans are also given the illusory perception of freedom by being farmed in the same way as free-range animals. We are allowed to roam unrestrained within our paddocks (nations), but at the same time are heavily governed by strict laws and regulations and are surrounded by fences that we call borders. We are deceived into believing that these are there for our own "security", but in truth they are there to keep us contained and controlled.

Just like in animal farming, we are also domesticated by the NHF's so that we become mentally and physically docile and obedient. OED defines domestication as, "*The process of taming an animal and keeping it as a pet or on a farm*", and they define the word "tame" as, "*Making something less powerful and easier to control*". This last definition cuts more directly to the true purpose of domestication and why it is used on us. Another advantage of domestication is that when we are born and raised by our domesticated parents, our lives as free-range humans within our captivity becomes so normalized and familiar that we never even think to question it. This also ensures that we do not even need to be domesticated directly by our masters, for our parents and environment do it naturally for them. This also causes us to develop the Stockholm Syndrome mentioned previously, whereby our captivity becomes so familiar that we become terrified at the thought of leaving it. We become convinced that life will be extremely dangerous without its control mechanisms "protecting" everyone and keeping "peace and order", and we even defend our masters if they are criticised.

There are four key ways in which we are domesticated and turned into free-range humans, all of which I have already alluded to throughout the book, but will touch on briefly again.

They are:

1. Our domestication process is initiated at birth by our already-domesticated parents and family, along with our surrounding cultural environment.

2. We are then sent to school, which in reality is a domestication factory designed to indoctrinate us into the ways of our native farm (country). Any instinctive behaviours that are difficult to control are conditioned out of us during this period as we are gradually tamed. Punishments and even drugs will even be administered if we resist, and our parents may be told that our "disobedient" behaviour is the result of a disorder. In truth, any resistance is just our natural instincts resisting the taming process. School also deliberately avoids teaching us anything that could be related to surviving in the world without the Cult, such as hunting, growing food, building shelter, finding water, and so on. This ensures that we become utterly dependent upon the Cult for our survival, just as a domesticated animal is dependent upon its captivity.

3. The Cult not only avoids teaching us the skills we require to survive on our own, but it has also taken control of nearly all of the resources that we require to survive. This again makes us utterly dependent on the Cult, and ensures that we will rarely

if ever entertain the idea of leaving the "security and safety" of our captivity.

4. Once we grow into a fully domesticated free-range adult human adequately prepared for a life in service to the Cult, we still remain subjected to a lifetime bombardment of propaganda designed to keep us hypnotised and in constant fear, anxiety, and stress.

CHAPTER 13

OCCULT ENTITIES—PARASITES OF THE MIND

Research has revealed that there exist two main factions of the NHF's who farm and feed off our lifeforce energy. The first faction is the ones that the Sumerians appeared to be referring to on their ancient tablets. These are higher density beings who can more easily project into our density and appear as physical beings, and are the ones who mostly control the Cabal and the Cult. It is widely believed that when in our density, many of these beings live and operate within deep underground military bases, commonly known as "DUMBs", where they run their human farming operation from. Countless abduction reports have revealed that when in their physical form they appear as reptilian-like beings, Greys, Nordic human-like beings, and mantid insect-like beings. The Mantid beings appear to be on the very top of the negative control hierarchy, with the Reptilians not far below on the pecking order. The Greys appear to be an artificially created robotic-like race, designed to serve the agenda of the Mantids and Reptilians in particular. These beings can also take possession of another person's body, especially if that person is a psychopath and therefore does not have a true Spirit occupying the body. What this means is that the members of the Cabal and their puppet leaders that we see on the world stage most often do not have a human soul or essence as we know it. Instead, their bodies are driven and controlled by much more negative and sinister beings, and these beings simply use them to mask their true identity and escape detection.

1: OCCULT ENTITIES

The second faction of NHF's is what are known as "occult entities", "demons", or "mind parasites". These are purely non-physical beings who could be considered the vultures or bottom feeders of the density above ours, that being Fourth Density.

What is similar in both factions is that the lifeforce energy of humans appears to be a particularly valuable food source for them and is their prime interest in us. Although the more physical beings also appear to be interested in other human resources such as our genetics, as well as Earth's valuable metals such as gold, platinum, and silver. In terms of extracting our lifeforce energy, the strategies utilised are different for each faction. The more physical NHF's relish consuming lifeforce energy in its purely energetic form, but can also consume it physically, such as in the form of human blood. The catch is that the blood must come from someone who is in a state of terror as it is extracted, as supposedly the adrenalin from the fear that enters into the blood is extremely nourishing to them. It is suspected that this blood is what is extracted in highly sadistic and secretive satanic rituals that occur within the Cabal circles and many of the upper levels of the Cult. Often these rituals utilise children, for supposedly the lifeforce energy of children is particularly pure and nourishing for these predators. This is why paedophilia and child-trafficking are rampant among the upper levels of the Cult, something that is becoming more well-known even among the general public. The famous late director Stanley Kubrick appeared to have been attempting to expose these secret Cult societies and their satanic rituals in his final ever film *Eyes Wide Shut*. Supposedly, the executives at Warner Bros demanded that 25 minutes of the film be removed, but Kubrick refused. Just four days later Kubrick died from an apparent "heart attack", and after his death the requested cuts were made just before the film's release. Clearly, what was cut from the film was very revealing, as the film was revealing enough even in its edited version.

In terms of how these more physical NHF's extract our lifeforce energy in its purely energetic form, abduction reports have uncovered them causing deliberate suffering to their victims and then lapping up the resulting energetic loosh with technological devices. Therefore, it appears they rely more upon technology to obtain their food, but how they do this on a large scale is up for debate. It has been theorised that they place cloaked ships or technological devices near areas of high suffering such as war zones, hospitals, funerals, and even sports stadiums. Sport has been turned into such a big spectacle within the Cult because the NHF's relish the emotionally charged energy from big sporting events, particularly the despair of the losing team. This is why they created the blood sports back in the days of the Romans, which is something they would still do publicly today if they could get away with it.

Occult entities (OE's), being purely non-physical, do not require physical food, meaning that they also do not require technology to obtain their food. Instead, they interfere with our thoughts and emotions and induce negative emotional states which they can feed off directly, and in this regard, they are true mind parasites. Tom Montalk explains how this occurs: *"As living human beings, we have not only physical bodies, but also etheric and astral bodies. The latter two comprise the soul. (Spirit is the seat of consciousness beyond the soul, and the soul acts as interface between spirit and body.) The more sentient OE's inhabit the astral plane in their native, weakened, or dormant state. There, they can affect us mentally and emotionally because our astral body extends into the astral plane. More specifically, it is the parts of our astral body that 'vibrate' at 'their level' that are amenable to their influence, which is why indulging in dark emotions, obsessions, and base passions increases one's vulnerability to their occult manoeuvres.*

"If an OE also acquires sufficient etheric energy, it can then condense for itself an etheric body and inhabit the etheric environment, meaning it then establishes a localized presence near the physical plane. At that point a clairvoyant can sense its presence in a certain part of a room, for instance. And if it gathers even more energy, it may even begin affecting things physically as seen in the poltergeist phenomenon. But if the OE grows too weak, it loses its grip on physicality and delocalizes back into the astral plane."

2: PREDATORS OF THE ASTRAL AND ETHERIC PLANES

OE's could be likened to the sharks of the astral and etheric planes, who circle around looking for their next prey. Being evil and demonic entities, they are vibrating on a level that is in harmony with suffering, cruelty, terror, and fear, and therefore, they are quite selective with who they target, preferring victims vulnerable to these states. People who emit these types of energies are similar to someone floating in the ocean whilst bleeding, which always attracts predators. However, OE's find us very difficult to detect when we are emitting positive emotional frequencies such as love, joy, and gratitude, when we think empowering thoughts, and when our bodies are clean and healthy. As a result, OE's will either hunt for prey that is more likely to provide them with the negative loosh they are after, or they will attempt to gradually lower someone's vibrational frequency through a series of attacks so that they become more vulnerable.

Montalk explains that, *"Prime targets include:*

- *Those who have been spiritually weakened by heavy drug or alcohol abuse.*
- *Those whose minds and souls have been fractured by trauma.*
- *The emotionally neurotic who are easily spooked.*
- *The psychically sensitive who are by definition more perceptive and responsive to, and thus manipulable by, the OE's audio, visual, and kinesthetic telepathic projections."*

Once they latch onto a target, the OE's exploit our traumas and emotionally vulnerable points by implanting thoughts of paranoia and insecurity into our minds, as well as inducing feelings of fear, depression, sadness, low energy, loneliness, insignificance, shame, anxiety, and temptations. An ideal outcome for the OE is to also lure us into engaging in self-destructive habits such as drug or alcohol abuse. This lowers our willpower and natural defences, making us more vulnerable to further attacks and exploitation. In fact, hijacking our habit circuits is one of their prime strategies, because they understand that we tend to be ruled by our daily habits. Being ruled by habits is not always a negative thing, for some people are ruled by positive habits, but if an OE can convert our daily habits into routines of self-sabotaging addictions, then they can begin controlling us like a puppet on a string. They also often use our natural sexual desires to tempt us to engage in promiscuous sex with strangers, as the act of sex can allow them to jump from body to body. This is especially the case if we engage in sex whilst intoxicated with drugs and alcohol, as the drugs lower our natural defences.

Overall, their primary goal is to create as much suffering within us as possible, which nourishes them with our lifeforce energy and builds their strength, but their end goal is a complete takeover (possession) of mind and body. Once a possession takes place, the OE can take our body around like a stolen car and wreak the maximum amount of havoc possible. Those people who are under the grips of deep addiction, paranoia, schizophrenia and depression, and who have constant voices in their heads, are most likely controlled if not fully possessed by an OE. This is why it is so difficult to reach people in these states because the real "them" is sadly enslaved within their own body. It takes a tremendous amount of effort and courage on our behalf if we wish to free ourselves from this position.

Unfortunately, many do not make it, as OE's also love to coax their victims into suicide, and they often succeed in doing so. This is advantageous for them, as suicide creates immense suffering in the victims' loved ones, which generates a banquet of food. The OE may lose its vehicle, but it had probably already drained its victim completely dry of his lifeforce energy anyway, and gained significant strength in the process. It can now simply hunt for a new victim.

A retired psychiatrist named Jerry Marzinsky has begun speaking publicly about his decades of experiences of working with schizophrenic patients in prisons and psychiatric hospitals. Marzinsky always assumed that the voices his patients heard in their heads were paranoid hallucinations. However, over time, Marzinsky began realising that these voices were in fact real, and were coming from demonic entities who were controlling and feeding off these people. Marzinsky's fascinating story can be heard on a podcast show titled *The Cosmic Matrix Podcast* with Marzinsky appearing on Episode 16, titled "Jerry Marzinsky—Schizophrenia, entities, and mental illness".

3: A GAME OF STEALTH

OE's primarily work through the blind spots that operate in our shadow, as their main objective is to go unnoticed whilst they carefully gain more and more control over our mind and body. If we knew they existed within our minds like parasites, we would be disgusted and resist their attacks. This is what inspired the legend of vampires, as just like OE's, vampires operate in the darkness, and in fact, vampires perish when they come into contact with sunlight. This is analogous to how OE's tend to immediately withdraw when we spot them and shine the light of our awareness onto them. The exceptions for this are when they have gained considerable strength and have taken possession of a body.

OE's remain hidden by planting thoughts and feelings of paranoia, fear, anxiety, and temptation into our mind and body that closely mimic our own style of thoughts and feelings, causing us to assume that they are our own. These thoughts and feelings are also carefully designed to trigger painful childhood wounds and Cult conditioning, producing powerful emotions that further cloud our judgment. As a result, we do not detect the predator in our midst and continue mechanically responding to these thoughts and feelings without discernment. The primary goal here for the OE is to have their target identify with these externally injected thoughts and feelings as if they are their own; this then produces the desired reaction and emotional state. For example, if we identify with an OE-injected thought of paranoia or insecurity, this will likely produce states of anxiety and fear. These states then produce the nourishing food that the OE's lap up. This not only strengthens the OE's, allowing them to attack us with even more power in the future, but it also weakens us in the process, causing us to become even more vulnerable to further attacks. As mentioned, once we find ourselves in this situation, with our lifeforce energies sapped and willpower weakened, and being controlled by an OE who grows stronger with every attack, escape is very difficult. This is especially the case if the OE has lured us into a variety of addictions. Typically, only a person with immense will power and desire to be free can unravel themselves from this situation.

If a person in this situation begins displaying signs of strength and resistance, the OE's, desperate not to lose a valuable source of food, will ferociously attack them in order to put them back in their place. The goal here is to pummel their victim into submission by attacking their every attempt to raise themselves up, eroding their self confidence in the process. Jerry Marzinsky witnessed firsthand how they did this to his patients. He explains that whenever his patients resisted the OE's commands, the OE's would attack them by implanting thoughts in their minds, such as telling them how pathetic they are, how nobody cares about them, how everyone thinks they're crazy, and how everything they do is worthless and will end in failure. The OE's would rely upon Marzinsky's patients identifying with these thoughts as if they were their own, which would cause them to become dejected and give up in their efforts of resistance.

Whilst OE's are attacking us, to further guarantee evading our detection, they can place a fog over our mind, ensuring that we can no longer think with any clarity. They also attempt to keep us distracted by the outer world so that we rarely if ever point our attention to our inner world where they reside. And they also rely on our collective assumption that the mind is a place of privacy and that nothing else can enter in there. Because most of us assume this to be true and never consider otherwise, we are never vigilant about observing and protecting our minds from external intrusions.

Highly respected philosopher Rudolf Steiner spoke at length about these beings, and over 100 years ago explained that, *"There are beings in the spiritual realms for whom anxiety and fear emanating from human beings offer welcome food. When humans have no anxiety and fear, then these creatures starve. People not yet sufficiently convinced of this statement could understand it to be meant comparatively only. But for those who are familiar with this phenomenon, it is a reality. If fear and anxiety radiate from people and they break out in panic, then these creatures find welcome nutrition and they become more and more powerful. These beings are hostile towards humanity.*

"Everything that feeds on negative feelings, on anxiety, fear and superstition, despair or doubt, are in reality hostile forces in supersensible worlds, launching cruel attacks on human beings, while they are being fed. Therefore, it is above all necessary to begin with that the person who enters the spiritual world overcomes fear, feelings of helplessness, despair and anxiety. But these are exactly the feelings that belong to contemporary culture and materialism; because it estranges people from the spiritual world, it is especially suited to evoke hopelessness and fear of the unknown in people, thereby calling up the above-mentioned hostile forces against them."

OE's particularly like to target those who are on the edge of an evolutionary leap of consciousness, meaning those who are becoming Spiritually embodied. They also seem to target those with high intelligence and who have a particular talent for inspiring and leading others. The reason for this is twofold. One, people of this nature typically have a high level of lifeforce energy emanating from them, and therefore, if they can become corrupted, they produce a particularly nourishing source of food. Secondly, these types of people are typically those who inspire others and help humanity as a collective experience evolutionary breakthroughs and leaps in consciousness. These are the people who produce breakthroughs in art, literature, philosophy, science, and leadership, all of which can catalyse a species to rapidly evolve. This type of evolution is the last thing that the OE's want, for if humanity evolves in consciousness, then our awareness will expand and we will begin perceiving them. This means that we will be much better prepared to protect ourselves and they will lose their food source. For this reason, OE's will attack and try to corrupt those who may have the potential to ignite an evolutionary leap forward in our species, and will seek to vector them away from their true potential.

Author Paul Levy explains that, "*These psychic vampires seek out people who are on the verge of a quantum, evolutionary leap in consciousness, but have not yet fully integrated their realizations and stabilized themselves in the higher, more coherent level of consciousness that they are beginning to access. These individuals are in an energetically sensitive and 'charged' condition, and their openness and vulnerability invites these vampiric entities to gorge on the light of their prey's expanding awareness, thereby preventing them from having enough energy to evolve to a higher level of consciousness. Like moths attracted to the light of a flame, these darker forces are particularly attracted to people who are actively engaged in consciousness raising activities, seeking truth, and speaking out about it with the intention of helping to awaken others.*

"*Whenever anyone would get too close to discovering their ploy, these parasitic entities would try—through their connections to the person's unconscious mind—to disorient them, diverting them from their path. For example, as we are on the verge of having a transformative and elusive insight, we might get distracted and fail to write it down, thereby not anchoring it to consciousness, and then afterwards forget—and lose—what we had realized. Or we might find ourselves, as we get close to seeing the covert psychological operations of the mind parasites, experiencing our unhealed trauma getting re-evoked, making us feel anxious or afraid. Or, as we begin to see through the subterfuge of these mind parasites, we might start feeling a lot of pain, which can easily cause us to dis-associate (i.e., split), resulting in moving away from our discovery of the mind parasites. Or we might suddenly have an overwhelming impulse to eat, or drink, or go for a walk—anything that would take us away from being present with what is happening in that moment. Or, as we begin to discover the light within ourselves, instead of cultivating an ever-deepening relationship with the radiance we find within, we might fall for the ruse of the mind parasites and identify with the light instead, becoming inflated and grandiose, thinking we are someone special. The mind parasites are masters of deception, tricksters par excellence. Though this can sound like the ravings of a paranoid madman, it is actually the opposite—a clear-sighted articulation of what we are up against.*"[42]

If we display traits of being particularly strong-willed, the OE's will attempt to break down our will power bit by bit, like an axeman chopping down a giant tree. They do this by constantly applying points of pressure upon our shadow wounds and vulnerabilities, especially things such as our unresolved traumas, cravings, desires, and addictions. The pressure they apply can range from being uncomfortable to nearly unbearable, and the intensity largely depends upon how vulnerable the weak point is and how strong our willpower is. For example, if we are in the midst of a battle with an addiction, then our willpower will be low and the pressure applied by the OE's to succumb to this addiction will feel deeply uncomfortable and difficult to resist. If, however, we consistently refuse to succumb to our addiction and our willpower grows in strength, then the OE attacks become more artful and subtle. For example, rather than tempt us back into our old addiction, they will instead try to tempt us into doing something that seems innocent and harmless, but which they intend to be a stepping stone to more self-destructive behaviours down the track. An example of this is someone who had addiction issues with recreational drugs. This person may have been clean for a while and has developed a strong will, and therefore cannot be easily lured back to his old drug habits. Therefore, the OE's will tempt him into something that seems innocent such as having a few drinks at a bar. Once intoxicated, his willpower will be lowered, which means the OE's can then lure him back to his old addictions more easily.

4: COMMON OE ATTACK STRATEGIES

OE's particularly like tempting us to use drugs and alcohol, because they cause our willpower and vibrational frequency to become lowered, making us more visible and vulnerable. On top of this, drugs and alcohol disembody us, especially when we are heavily intoxicated, which means our body basically becomes an empty vehicle that an OE can take for a joyride. This is especially the case in crowded bars and clubs where OE's can jump from body to body. Most people have likely had experiences where they have been so intoxicated that they can't remember what occurred, and in which they also committed embarrassing actions that they otherwise would never have done. This is because something "else" took over in those periods of unconsciousness. Alternatively, many people have experienced being so intoxicated that it appeared as if they were possessed, and this is because they most likely were.

OE's also like to strike when we are fatigued and emotionally overwhelmed, as this is when our defences are down. For this reason, they often target us in our dreams by inducing nightmares or by planting certain negative commands into our subconscious mind. This causes us to have broken and poor-quality sleeps, leaving us drained and vulnerable during the day. If we ever awaken in the morning feeling sad, depressed, and/or exhausted, despite having slept for our normal length of time, it is likely that we were targeted in our sleep.

OE's may even appear in our dreams as angelic beings in order to be more easily accepted and trusted, as this is one of their favourite and most well utilised deceptions. Many psychics, clairvoyants, and channelers, who are communicating with and passing on messages from higher density entities, are commonly deceived by this. They may believe that they are communicating with positive beings such as angels or highly evolved spirits, but are in fact more often than not communicating with OE's in disguise. OE's can also appear as visions to people under the influence of psychedelics such as Ayahuasca or LSD, once again posing themselves as angelic beings. If we fall for these deceptions, we will invite them into our lives, and they begin a series of more serious and harmful attacks. For this reason, we must always remain vigilant and remember that these beings are the masters of deception.

One of Sri Aurobindo's top students, who went by the name of Satprem, shares a relevant quote regarding the OE's: "*They are highly conscious forces whose sole aim, apparently, is to discourage the seeker and divert him from the path he has chosen. The first sign of their presence is easily perceptible: joy is clouded, consciousness is clouded, everything becomes shrouded in an atmosphere of melodrama and gloom. Personal distress is a sure sign of the enemy's presence. Melodrama is a favorite haunt of these forces; that is how they are able to create the greatest havoc, because they play with a very old teammate within us, who cannot help loving melodrama even as he cries out for relief. First, they generally make a point of forcing us into sudden, extreme, and irrevocable decisions in order to take us as far away as possible from our path – a pressing, exacting vibration that demands immediate compliance; or else, they take apart, with remarkable skill, the whole system of our quest to prove that we are deluding ourselves and that our efforts will come to nothing; more often, they bring about a state of depression, playing with another well-known teammate within us whom Sri Aurobindo calls the man of sorrows: a fellow . . . covering himself with a sevenfold overcoat of tragedy and gloom, and he would not feel his existence justified if he couldn't be colossally miserable. All the vibrations of disorder that we call "our" sorrow or "our" troubles have the immediate result of weakening or disintegrating our protective "field of snow,"* (our 'aura', Authors note) *which means that the door is wide open to the adverse forces. They have a thousand and one ways of attacking us – for we are indeed under attack – and the more determined we are, the more relentless they become. This may seem like an exaggeration but only one who has never tried to make progress would doubt it. As long as we move with the common herd, life is relatively easy, with its moderate ups and downs; but the moment we want to get out of the rut, a thousand forces rise up, suddenly very interested that we should behave "like everyone else," then we realize how well organized the imprisonment is.*

These adverse forces have been given all sorts of devilish and "negative" names through the world's spiritual history, as if their sole aim were to damn the seeker and give decent people a hard time.

The method for dealing with these adverse forces is the same as for the other vibrations: silence, inner stillness that lets the storm blow over. We may not succeed the first time in dissolving these attacks, but more and more they will seem to take place on the surface of our being; we may be shaken, upset, yet deep down we will feel the "Witness" in us, unscathed and unaffected – he is never affected. We fall and get back up again, each time becoming stronger. The only sin is discouragement."

As mentioned earlier, the most nourishing and powerful food OE's (and all NHF's for that matter) can obtain is the loosh derived from children. Supposedly, once we go through puberty, our lifeforce energy undergoes vibrational changes that makes it less potent for the OE's, although it is still highly nourishing. This is why OE's particularly like to possess the bodies of people who are in positions of power and who have direct access to children. This is why there are so many allegations and convictions of child rape and paedophilia within institutions such as the Church and Hollywood, among many other industries. Many examples of this have been hitting the mainstream media in recent times, and yet what we have heard is only the tip of the iceberg compared to some of the unimaginably dark and evil things that are occurring. Many such dark happenings will eventually be brought into the light for all to see, which is what must occur in order to trigger a large-scale Spiritual embodiment process within humanity.

5: THE HUMAN AURIC FIELD – OUR NATURAL DEFENCE

In order to make their attacks effective, an OE must first ensure that they can penetrate our auric field, which is a naturally occurring EMF field that surrounds our body, protecting us from psychic attacks. This is similar to how the skin protects us from allowing unwanted parasites into the body. In a healthy individual, with all the natural conditions of health being met, the auric field should be strong and provide adequate protection. This is why OE's tempt us into habits that damage our auric field, such as abusing drugs, alcohol, junk foods, and experiencing chronic stress. Once our auric field has been damaged, OE's can then penetrate through and impose a heavier influence over our thoughts, feelings, and behaviours, and begin controlling us like a puppet on strings. The Cult supports this process of damaging our auric field by engineering an environment wherein we are relentlessly bombarded by toxins and stress. The NHF-controlled Cabal have achieved this by putting fluoride with its heavy metal contaminants in the public water supply, creating addictive junk and genetically modified foods, normalising the regular consumption of alcohol, stimulants, and drugs, poisoning the air with chemtrails, treating us with pharmaceuticals disguised as "medicines", injuring the still developing nervous system in children with toxic vaccines, and creating a highly competitive and economically driven culture, just to name a few of many such examples. The next big threat to the human auric field that is just around the corner is the rollout of the 5G wireless Internet grid, which will permanently bathe humanity in highly potent radiation.

The following is a list of some key requirements, from a mental, spiritual, and physical perspective, that support a healthy and strong mind, body, and auric field, thus largely protecting us against attacks from both the semi-physical and non-physical NHF's. The NHF's also understand these requirements and that is why they have created an artificial environment (the Cult) that has successfully attacked and corrupted each and every one of them. Therefore, it is crucial that we take it upon ourselves to ensure that these key areas are sufficiently met within our personal lives to the best of our ability. This is a great task that may take many years to accomplish, and requires supreme efforts, determination, courage, and focus. What must also be understood is that the goal here is not perfection, but balance. The reality is that by the time most of us awaken, there will already have been damage caused to our body and auric field as a result of being subjected to a lifetime of NHF attacks and Cult based programming. The amount of damage we have suffered will determine the amount of effort required to regain our full health and strength, which of course will vary greatly from person to person. Luckily, however, Nature has endowed us with a highly durable and resilient body and auric field. This means that unless the damage is too deep and irreversible, full health and strength can nearly always be regenerated as long as the right conditions are provided.

These key requirements are;

- Not being exposed to poisons in the mother's womb whilst a developing foetus, which requires a non-drug using and generally healthy mother.
- A natural birthing process free from traumas such as circumcision and vaccinations.
- A diet of healthy mother's milk for as long as necessary, until natural wholefoods can be digested.
- A childhood free from significant emotional and physical traumas.
- A close and tight-knit family unit that supports and loves each other.
- A significant amount of attention, emotional nurturing, and physical touch as a child.
- Copious amounts of unbridled time to play and explore Nature as a child.
- Plenty of solitude as a child (and adult) in order to begin to understand and know oneself.
- Clean and natural water free from fluoride and heavy metals.
- Adequate amounts of sunshine and fresh air, and regular sunbathing over the entire nude body. The sun is crucial in maintaining a healthy and strong body and auric field, which is why the sun has been so demonised by the Cult. The Cabal are even trying to block out the sun via what they call 'geoengineering'.
- A nourishing diet consisting of wholefoods free from chemical pesticides and grown in rich, fertile soil, as well as meat and animal products that have been either wild caught or raised in

natural pastures and have not received added hormones and chemicals.

- Daily exercising and stretching.
- Daily doses of grounding in Nature, with the bare feet touching the earth.
- Daily meditation, with a particular focus on embodiment practises.
- A social environment that encourages one to pursue creative passions with unbridled enthusiasm.
- A social environment that does not breed stress and anxiety, and does not invade privacy.
- Freedom from all addictions.
- Adequate daily rest and sleep, free from the influence of the EMF pollution that emanates from wireless technologies.
- A close-knit social community and tribe that supports and provides emotional healing and nurturing to each other.
- An education that includes a deep study of Nature and how to be resourceful within it, such as finding water, growing food, building shelter, building community, etc.
- An education that includes a study and understanding of the spiritual realms and the different beings that inhabit them, as well as a study of all of the topics raised in this book.

6: SELF-VIGILANCE

On top of the requirements just mentioned, another key to protecting ourselves from OE attacks is by learning to become vigilant in observing the inner mechanisms of our mind. This is in contrast to being constantly distracted by the happenings of the external world, which is what the OE's want. By doing this, we can learn to discern which thoughts and feelings are truly ours and which have been externally injected into us. This can be difficult at first, but with practise and by awakening Spirit, it becomes easier and more natural. One tell-tale sign that a thought and feeling is not our own is by the suddenness that it strikes us with. An external injection will feel like an attack, as it will come on suddenly and without any warning. It may manifest as a sudden bout of anxiety, fear, or even anger toward another person. Or it may manifest as an intense feeling of depression, doubt, paranoia, and insecurity about our self. Again, what the OE hopes for in these circumstances is for us to become identified with the injected thought or feeling, and therefore react mechanically to it. In the case of anxiety or depression, the OE hopes for us to reach for a coping mechanism such as a drug, or to binge eat junk food, which then lowers our willpower and auric field, making us vulnerable to further attacks. Or, in the case of being injected with anger toward another person, the OE hopes for us to project that anger and then initiate a conflict. Or, in the case of paranoia and self-doubt, the OE hopes that we will start belittling ourselves, which will lower our self-confidence, strength, and willpower, again making us more vulnerable to further attacks. Or, the OE may even plant belittling thoughts directly into our minds, in the hope that they will erode our self-belief. The key in these circumstances is to simply observe what we are thinking and feeling without identifying or reacting mechanically.

Eventually, the uncomfortable feelings that the attack triggered within us will begin to fade and then leave. However, if we identify and respond mechanically to these thoughts and feelings, such as projecting our anger onto another person and creating a conflict, it will only serve to draw out our suffering. As well, being merely reactive signals to the OE's that we are vulnerable to attacks, and we then attract more of them into our lives. Learning to maintain self-control and remain neutral when under an OE attack is something that requires will power and a high level of self-awareness, and also takes time and patience. It is a skill that becomes stronger and more resilient overtime, and will likely require a number of failed attempts in order to highlight where our vulnerabilities lie.

Eventually, we can develop our self-awareness and willpower to the point whereby the OE's largely leave us alone. One key reason for this is that the OE's must operate from the shadows, as our direct awareness of them appears to repel them. In fact, the way in which they are so desperate to avoid our detection makes one wonder if the light of our awareness is poisonous to them. Regardless, what this means is that the more self-aware we are as a result of shadow work, and the more we vigilantly watch our own mind and are on guard against external attacks, the less space the OE's have in which to attack.

Although, even if we have largely integrated our shadow, the OE's do not leave us alone permanently, and their attacks certainly do not cease. This is because no one can be fully self-aware and vigilant at all times, and understanding this, the OE's wait patiently for their opportunity to strike. This opportunity will come for them as soon as we lose vigilance, which occurs whenever we become mechanical and identified with the ego personality.

Their attacks will also become more cunning and subtle, and they will even resort to attacking us through other people, utilising anyone who is asleep and unconscious as their puppet. For this, they particularly like to utilise those closest to us, such as a romantic partner, close friend, or family members, because the emotional bonds we have with them serve to make the attacks more painful and difficult to cope with. An example of this could be someone who is waking up to the truth about the Cult and OE attacks, but who lives in a family that is still under the spell of the Cult. As she learns to become resilient to OE attacks herself, the OE's may instead work through her parents and use them as portals to attack her. To initiate these attacks, the OE's may inject feelings of fear and anger into her parents' minds regarding the path their daughter is taking, which will likely cause them to project their fear and anger on to her in a way that leads to conflict.

7: DIVIDE & CONQUER

OE's also love to resort to Machiavellian techniques to create conflict between people, and they are exceptionally cunning in how they achieve this. In the example just used, whilst the OE's are using the parents as portals to attack their daughter, they will also be injecting intense feelings of hurt and rejection into the daughter's mind. Their goal is to amplify the pain she is feeling from being attacked by the people she thought would support her. This may also cause her to react with anger and create even further conflict. If successful, a banquet of loosh will be produced that the OE's can feed off, as well causing the daughter to doubt the path of awakening she is taking. The key to protecting oneself in these situations is to develop firm boundaries that others cannot cross, and not to tolerate attacks from anyone, even if they are close family and friends. This is not a suggestion to respond with anger or violence, but simply to stand one's ground in a calm and measured way. This can be very hard when we are attacked by people that we are emotionally connected to, but what must be remembered is that it is often not truly "them" who are doing the attacking.

Another crucial element of becoming resilient to OE attacks is to resist falling into victim mode. The truth is that OE's are part of the fabric of reality, and there is nothing "wrong" with them, nor can they be eliminated, for they are performing a specific function given to them by the Great Spirit. They are like the predators and parasites we find here on Earth who have their natural place in the greater wholeness of Nature; but they instead inhabit the lower levels of Fourth density. Through their attacks, the OE's unwittingly provide us with a beneficial service. This is because as mentioned, the OE's only attack us through the blind spots that lie hidden within our shadow. This means that each attack serves as an opportunity for us to become aware of something within our shadow that we were previously blind to. Using their attacks as feedback mechanisms, we can utilise them as valuable tools to aid us in our shadow integration and Spiritual embodiment process.

This points to the higher function given to the OE's by the Great Spirit, which is to help us awaken and become spiritually embodied by highlighting our blind spots with each attack. This service, however, is only available to those who are willing to confront their shadow and take responsibility for their Spiritual embodiment process. If, instead, we remain in victim mode and fall into the trap of shadow projection, we will not learn anything, and will simply attract more attacks. But, if we do learn from the OE attacks and become resistant to them, the lifeforce energy that was previously being manipulated and siphoned from us, instead remains there for us to utilise. This fills us with immense strength and power, allowing us to become even stronger in resisting their attacks, as well as becoming strong enough to support others as well.

Satprem speaks of the higher function of these forces in the following passage, *"In reality, as experience shows, these disturbing forces have their place in the universe; they are disturbing only at the scale of our constricted momentary consciousness, and for a specific purpose. Firstly, they always catch us with our defenses down—yet were we firm and one-pointed, they could not shake us for a second. In addition, if we look into ourselves instead of whining and blaming the devil or the world's wickedness, we find that each of these attacks has exposed one of our many virtuous pretenses...*

"For the individual as for the world, these rather ungracious forces are instruments of progress. 'By what men fall, by that they rise,' says the Kularnava Tantra in its wisdom. We protest against the apparently useless and arbitrary "catastrophe" that strikes our heart or our flesh, and we blame the 'Enemy,' but is it not possible that the soul itself—not the outward mind, but the spirit within has accepted and chosen these things as part of its development in order to get through the necessary experience at a rapid rate, to hew through, durchhauen, even at the risk or the cost of much damage to the outward life and the body? To the growing soul, to the spirit within us, may not difficulties, obstacles, attacks be a means of growth, added strength, enlarged experience, training for spiritual victory?"

CHAPTER 14

THE NEW WORLD ORDER

"Do you begin to see, then, what kind of world we are creating? It is the exact opposite of the stupid hedonistic Utopias that the old reformers imagined. A world of fear and treachery is torment, a world of trampling and being trampled upon, a world which will grow not less but more merciless as it refines itself. Progress in our world will be progress towards more pain. The old civilizations claimed that they were founded on love or justice. Ours is founded upon hatred. In our world there will be no emotions except fear, rage, triumph, and self-abasement. Everything else we shall destroy, everything. Already we are breaking down the habits of thought, which have survived from before the Revolution. We have cut the links between child and parent, and between man and man, and between man and woman. No one dares trust a wife or a child or a friend any longer. But in the future there will be no wives and no friends. Children will be taken from their mothers at birth, as one takes eggs from a hen. The sex instinct will be eradicated. Procreation will be an annual formality like the renewal of a ration card. We shall abolish the orgasm. Our neurologists are at work upon it now. There will be no loyalty, except loyalty towards the Party. There will be no love, except the love of Big Brother."

~*1984*, by George Orwell

Whilst the Cult already has immense power and control over the human race, it has not yet achieved its objectives in terms of where it wishes to take us, although it is certainly close. The agenda it wishes to play out is extremely important to understand, because we are still within a small window of opportunity whereby we can influence and change the direction it is heading. However, if it is allowed to play out to its completion as planned, then escape is going to be very difficult, if not impossible. What is clear is that the NHF-controlled Cabal are not satisfied with the way their global human farming operation is being managed. From their perspective, there is still too much freedom and potential for escape available to us, and to counteract this, they are desperate to lock us down into an inescapable technological prison. This prison is what they have been publicly labelling as the "New World Order" (NWO).

The outline of the NWO is unimaginably sinister, as it includes targets such as:

- *A significant population reduction.* This is already well underway.
- *A segregation of humans into what will be known as "human settlement zones" with tremendous blocks of land being labelled as "forbidden zones".* Humans will not be permitted to live or even enter into these forbidden zones of natural habitat, which will be very large in size.
- *A complete segregation between the super wealthy elite (the 1%) and the other 99% of humanity (already well achieved).* What we have known as the middle class will (and already is) being dismantled and will be placed on the same level as the 99%. This is being achieved largely through manipulations of the economy. The Cabal will likely engineer another major stock market crash within the next 5-10 years (or sooner), which they will capitalise on to buy up much of the assets of the middle class (particularly land and property) and drain them of their wealth. This exact scenario has already occurred many times in the past, as is documented in methodical detail in *The Creature from Jekyll Island.* The most recent occurrence was the deliberately engineered global financial crash of 2008. Even Hollywood revealed the manipulation behind this crash in the 2015 movie *The Big Short* starring Brad Pitt and Christian Bale.
- *Everything in society* to be *controlled and regulated by artificial intelligence (AI).* AI is being cleverly infused into our lives through our "smart" devices, which is only the beginning.

- *Confusing people about their gender so as to create a race of people without identity, causing them to become much more likely to look to authority to give them their identity instead.* This part of the agenda is not about supporting people who identity with a different gender than the body they are in, such as a person in a male body identifying as a woman, which of course is everyone's right to do so if they wish. This is about confusing people about their gender, especially young children, who otherwise weren't confused and weren't even thinking about it. This aspect of the agenda is already well underway and is the reason why gender identity and fluidity are beginning to be taught to young children in classrooms.

- *Natural births to become a thing of the past with humans eventually being born inside artificial wombs.* This ties into the gender identity point above. The goal is to remove gender identity, conditioning future human generations to identify as being 'gender neutral' or 'gender fluid'. Meaning that they identify as neither man nor woman. This will eventually cause them to cease seeing themselves as the creators of the next generation of babies, and they will fully support babies being born inside artificial wombs instead. This will allow each new generation- to be raised, programmed, conditioned, and genetically modified by the Cabal from embryo to adult, giving them complete and nearly irreversible control over humanity. These artificially born children will likely undergo specific trauma-based mind control and behavioural conditioning techniques designed to make them completely subservient to their masters, exactly as depicted in Aldous Huxley's *Brave New World*. Humans will also likely be sterilised so that they can never give birth, and it will become normal for woman to have had their uteruses removed. Major attempts to sterilise humanity have already been taking place for many decades, which have been very successful. If humanity becomes completely sterilised, there will be no other options but to create babies artificially, which of course is the plan. This part of the agenda may sound farfetched to some, but as mentioned previously, scientists have already developed artificial wombs that they have been testing on prematurely birthed foetal lambs, with the target of eventually developing them for human use. To most people, allowing their child to be born and raised in an artificial womb is unimaginable and is something they would never allow. What we must understand is that the Cabal programs the minds of each generation differently, and future generations will be raised to think that growing humans artificially is just "normal", and even "logical". We accept many things as "normal" today that previous generations never would have imagined or accepted. Things such as having surveillance cameras all over public spaces, needing permits to capture fresh rainwater, and mandatory vaccines, just to name a few of countless such examples. We accept these as normal today because the Cabal have very clever methods of programming each generation in ways that negate any resistance to their agenda.

- *A blending of all the races so that any unique and independent national, racial, and cultural identity is taken out of humanity.* This is being achieved through deliberately engineered immigrations, which have been orchestrated to create what the Cabal call a "melting pot". A melting pot is a nation full of such a vast variety and blend of different cultures that no distinguishable culture remains. The purpose of creating a melting pot in every nation is so that the Cabal can then more easily integrate all nations into one global nation, which will be governed by a one-world government which they control. The reason they need to create a melting pot to achieve this, is because nations with strong independent values, traditional culture, and national pride have always historically resisted the Cabal. This is because these values and traditions give the people something that they believe to be very important to preserve and protect. Therefore, mixing many cultures together within a nation ensures old values and traditions are slowly forgotten, meaning that the people of that nation have little to nothing left to preserve and fight for. This guarantees that they will provide little resistance when the Cabal begin to absorb their country into the single global nation.

This melting pot is currently being achieved under the guise of increasing the 'racial diversity' within every country. Whilst this sounds like a nice humanitarian slogan on the surface, in truth it is an empty platitude designed to mask what the Cabal truly wish to create. What they actually intend is for the complete destruction of diversity, with diversity instead being replaced with widespread uniformity. They intend to, and already are, melting every culture together, so that each unique culture can then be systematically destroyed together. Once destroyed, all cultures will be morphed into one subservient rootless culture, meaning each culture will have lost all connection with their roots and have forgotten who they are and where they came from. This includes losing connection with their ancestors, traditions, customs, science, religion, and spiritual beliefs, just to name a few. Once again, this agenda is already well advanced and under way, with the melting pot and rootless culture they wish to create being what we know of as 'Western culture'. This is why so called 'Western culture' is like a disease that is spreading across the world, corrupting the culture and lives of the people in every country it reaches. The disease aspect of Western culture comes from the toxicity engineered into it by the Cabal themselves. Success in this plan requires a slow and gradual melting of the races and cultures in a way whereby they do not unite and rebel against those manipulating them. In order to further prevent a united rebellion, the Cabal engineers divide and conquer tactics to create tension between the different racial and cultural factions as they're being melted together. However, if each race and culture can realise that everyone is being manipulated equally, then there is a chance that there could still be a unified resistance. This requires people understanding the Machiavellian techniques being used on them.

- *A one-world nation, controlled by a totalitarian one-world government, protected by a world army, funded by a world bank, with every citizen microchipped, and everything and everyone on the entire planet under permanent surveillance monitoring and AI control.* Again, already well advanced.

CHAPTER 15

THE NWO END GAME: SOCIAL CREDITING SYSTEM, 5G, AND TRANSHUMANISM

"The illusion of freedom will continue as long as it's profitable to continue the illusion. At the point where the illusion becomes too expensive to maintain, they will just take down the scenery, they will pull back the curtains, they will move the tables and chairs out of the way and you will see the brick wall at the back of the theater."

~Frank Zappa

1: THE SOCIAL CREDIT SYSTEM

One key objective of the NWO agenda is to gradually implement a technologically controlled system known as the "Social Crediting System" (SCS) into every country. How the SCS will operate is that all tangible money will be eliminated and replaced by a digital currency, which will be likely known as "social credit". We will also be provided with a social rating score, and both the amount of social credits we receive, and our social rating score, will be based upon our social behaviour. Our social rating score will be calculated by the central AI, which will give us an average rating out of 5. Part of the preparation for gradually implementing this SCS has been to first introduce corporations like Uber and Airbnb into societies, which use this very same rating system.

When the SCS is introduced, what we will be judged on overall is our level of obedience to the rules of the SCS, and this will be determined by analysing things such as our social media posts and interactions, criminal and driving history, credit rating, shopping purchases, and general surveillance footage. The surveillance footage, however, will be much more intensive that what we are accustomed to today. For when the SCS is online, AI controlled surveillance cameras will be monitoring every square inch of society, as well as monitoring us through every smart device. An online article summarises this system well: *"Imagine a world where an authoritarian government monitors everything you do, amasses huge amounts of data on almost every interaction you make, and awards you a single score that measures how 'trustworthy' you are. In this world, anything from defaulting on a loan to criticising the ruling party, from running a red light to failing to care for your parents properly, could cause you to lose points. And in this world, your score becomes the ultimate truth of who you are—determining whether you can borrow money, get your children into the best schools or travel abroad; whether you get a room in a fancy hotel, a seat in a top restaurant—or even just get a date."*[43]

An eerie episode of the British show *Black Mirror* depicts how this SCS world will likely operate. In Episode 1 of Season 3, titled "Nosedive", a futuristic world is portrayed whereby a SCS is in full effect. In this world, each person wears AI-infused contact "smart" lenses, which analyses the data of each person one comes into contact with. For example, when the main character of the show bumps into a friend on the street, her smart lenses show her the other person's social rating score and any other associated personal data. This allows her to know if she is in contact with someone of a high or low social rating. Then, after this interaction, she must rate the other person out of 5, and the other person must also rate her. In fact, each person must rate each other after every single interaction, no matter how minor or meaningless it was. As a result, the main character must be on her best social behaviour *at all times* if she wishes to maintain a high social rating score. A high score is important because it determines her standing in society, and whether or not she can receive a good loan, get a well-paid job, or even eat in certain restaurants.

To many, this type of system may sound unimaginable, but this exact SCS has already been introduced in China and will be fully online there by 2020. What this means, in terms of the NHF's global farming operation, is that the farm paddock that we know of as China has been prepped to accept this new system without resistance sooner than the other farm paddocks. Investigating how the Chinese SCS will operate provides us with an eerie glimpse as to how it will operate everywhere, as China has been a testing ground for the Cabal. Now they intend on slowly implementing the Chinese system all over the world, and in fact, this is already well under way.[44]

Many people will find it hard to accept that this system will be implemented outside of China, because China is known as an openly communist country. Whereas, most other countries are supposedly democratic and are given the "choice" of who will lead them and how they will be led. It is important to remember that this choice is just an illusion, and that the same Cabal are always ruling in the background no matter which puppet is "elected" into power, or which system is implemented. What we call "communism" is just a name for a system that the Cabal uses to control the masses, one that historically has been very effective in achieving this aim. What we currently have in our "democratic" societies is "capitalism", which despite being a system that supposedly stands for personal freedom and independence, eventually achieves the same results as communism. That being a society completely controlled and owned by the state, which occurs mostly because the Cabal have hijacked and corrupted capitalism with their Federal Reserve banking system.

The only issue with capitalism from the perspective of the Cabal is that even despite their manipulations, it still provides too much freedom and independence to the individual. Communism, however, is a system in which the Cabal can control the masses more completely, openly, and without rebellion, and demand total uniformity and obedience to the state. For this reason, they wish to spread communism all over the world, but they wish for this modern form of communism to be controlled technologically, which is the purpose of the SCS. Knowing most people's disdain for communism, the Cabal have been slowly and gradually infiltrating it into our current systems in ways that most remain unawares to. They will continue this covert subjugation until the point of no return has been reached, in which it will then become very much out in the open for all to see.[45]

When the SCS is online, those of us who are disobedient to its rules will be deducted credits and will have our social rating score lowered, and such disobedient behaviour will be given an Orwellian term such as "untrustworthy social behaviour". If we display "untrustworthy social behaviour" on a frequent basis, we will then have our social credit account suspended. In this system, social credits will be required to access nearly everything; therefore, having our account suspended will mean an exclusion from society. To ensure everything in society is fully reliant on the use of credits, the Cabal also intend to introduce what is known as the "Smart Grid" and the "Internet of Things" (IOT). The Smart Grid and IOT are technological systems in which all devices will be converted into "smart devices", and these smart devices will be connected by a central AI. Smart devices will include everything from the toaster, shower, toilet, fridge, car to public technologies like trains, trams, busses, and so on. So-called futurists have even spoken about the human body and plant life being eventually connected to the Smart Grid through nanotechnology. All of our everyday devices, once converted to smart devices, will require the payment of social credits every time we wish to use them. Many will even require us to have a certain social rating if we wish to use them, or they will offer extra conveniences for those with a high social rating score. For example, public transport systems such as trains and buses will contain seats only available to those with social rating scores of 4.97/5 or higher. Or, whenever there are queues at the airport, or other public spaces, those with high social rating scores can use the priority line.

As part of the incremental introduction of these systems into each country, most public transport systems are already set up in a similar way. Here in Australia, to get on a train we must place digital credits onto our train card and then tap that card on a machine before entering the platform. If we have enough credits, we receive a green light to say that we can access the train; if we do not have enough credits, then we are given a red light to indicate that we do not have access. Once the IOT and Smart Grid are online, everything will operate this way, from the smaller devices like a toaster or a fridge, to larger things like a train or a plane. This means that if our social credit account is either suspended, does not have enough credits available, or if we have a low social rating score, then we will automatically be blocked from using all of the technology that our lives now rely on. This already occurs today whereby if we have a bad credit rating then we can't apply for a loan, or, if we do not have enough credits on our train card then we cannot use the train. All of this is by design to prepare us for the coming SCS, but when this system is online, it will be applied to nearly every single interaction we have with every device on the planet. There will be no room to argue, either, as it will be a binary green light (yes) or red light (no) based system only.

The Cabal plan on having this entire system governed and controlled by a world-wide central AI, and they wish to remove all human-to-human interactions and replace them with human-to-AI interactions only. For example, currently, if we have issues with something like accessing a plane or train, we can generally speak to another person and find a resolution. In the future, once the SCS has been implemented, this will no longer be a possibility. The AI will give us either a green light or a red light, and because it is AI rather than a real person, there will be no room to argue or reason with it. The only option will be to obey no matter how much we do not like it or how unjust it is. The Cabal will write the backend algorithms that will program which rules the AI will enforce within the SCS, which will provide them with ultimate social control.

This also means that if the Cabal wanted to make a sweeping change in society, they can simply write and upload a new algorithm into the AI. For example, if too many people are speaking out against government, the Cabal can program an algorithm that commands the AI to suspend the social credit accounts of anyone caught doing this. There will be cameras and microphones littered in every square inch of society, unmanned drones flying in the air, and microphones and cameras within every smart device, all connected to the central AI. This will give the Cabal unprecedented surveillance over humanity, meaning it will be nearly impossible to disobey the strict algorithms that they will write.

Even when the AI suspends our social credit account for something arbitrary, minor, and unjust, there will be very little to nothing we can do about it, as there will be no opportunity for complaint or appeal. If our account is suspended, we will be labelled by the AI as an "untrustworthy" citizen, and this label will likely appear on the screen of every device that we attempt to use, along with "access denied". It is also likely that we will be placed on a period of strict probation, whereby we must receive zero strikes in order to be labelled "trustworthy" once again. Or, if we become repeat "offenders", then we will likely be forced into what they will call "social rehabilitation" or some other similar Orwellian term. Someone in social rehabilitation will be made to appear to others as someone who is dangerous, and a threat to social peace and order. In social rehabilitation, the "offender" will likely undergo severe mind control programming and behavioural conditioning, and will be placed on a cocktail of pharmaceuticals, in order to pummel them back into blind obedience. Once, or if, they re-enter society, with their will power broken, their mind reprogrammed, and drugged into docility, they will be praised by others as having been "rehabilitated".

A great example of how this SCS will function can be seen in the 1993 movie *Demolition Man* starring Sylvester Stallone, Wesley Snipes, and Sandra Bullock. In this movie, society is strictly controlled by a technologically based totalitarian system, and a central AI issues warning tickets and punishments for anyone caught disobeying the rules. In humorous scenes, Stallone's character is issued warnings by the AI every time he uses a swear word. In this world, even physical human touch such as kissing and having sex, as well as listening to music, have all been made illegal. This sounds extreme, but this level of control is what is eventually planned for us.

Another example of how the AI controlled IOT and Smart Grid will operate can be found in the *Iron Man* movies starring Robert Downey Jr. In these movies, Downey's lead character Tony Stark's entire house consists of smart devices (a Smart Grid) that are connected by a central AI known as Jarvis. Through this Smart Grid, Stark can speak to Jarvis and ask it to do anything he needs, which is how the entire world will operate once the SCS and Smart Grid is online. The difference is that in the *Iron Man* movies, this system is depicted as cool and futuristic, and provides an immense amount of power and convenience to Stark. As well, the voice of Jarvis is made to sound perfectly human, personable, and even humorous, rather than artificial and robotic, and Jarvis and Stark relate to each other as if they are old friends.[46] This is a classic Hollywood programming tool called pre-emptive programming. This is where a depiction of a potential future is programmed into our minds so that when it begins to be tiptoed into society, it is already familiar to us, and therefore, we are much less likely to resist it. Also, by portraying this technology as being cool, fun, personable, non-threatening, and powerful, not only will we not resist it, but many will welcome and encourage it.

The rules imposed onto us by the SCS will be extremely strict, and these will all be implemented in the name of "social peace, order, trust, and security". These rules will ensure that any questioning of authority, even if it is a criticism of an abuse or atrocity, will lead to a deduction of credits or an account suspension. This means that eventually we will be punished for behaviours that we currently perceive as basic human rights, such as freedom of speech, which is something that is already occurring today.

Eventually, even certain emotions and thoughts will be made illegal, and there will be technologies that will be able to scan us and analyse what we are thinking and feeling based on our body's biorhythms. In fact, such technologies are already being developed.[47] A Hollywood movie released in 2015 titled *Equals*, starring Kristen Stewart, depicted a dystopian world in which human emotions are outlawed and are considered to be symptoms of a disease known as "Switched on Syndrome". Everyone in society must therefore take a drug each day to prevent the onset of this syndrome, and anyone displaying symptoms are forced to enter a rehabilitation facility known as the DEN (Defective Emotional Neuropathy) Facility. Here they undergo severe pharmaceutical-based mind programming "treatment". In this world, emotions are thought of in a similar vein as to how we currently perceive diseases like diabetes or cancer. As well, human touch and sex are forbidden, and women are instead artificially inseminated in order to become pregnant. This movie was another clear attempt to either warn humanity about what is to come or to prepare our minds for its eventual arrival.

Those who will be heavily targeted by the rules of the SCS will be people who are disobedient to authority, people who criticise government, and people who are creative and inventive in their thinking. The goal will be to limit the freedom of these types of people to the point whereby they have very little influence on society. They will even be portrayed as being mentally and emotionally unstable, and disruptive to social peace and order. On the other hand, those who follow the rules imposed by the SCS with enthusiasm and obedience will be rewarded with extra social credits, a high social rating score, and extra privileges and luxuries.

This is already occurring in China, whereby millions of Chinese citizens have been banned from certain privileges because of their social behaviour. For example, 9 million Chinese have been banned from being able to purchase domestic flights, among many other restrictions.[48] China will also focus on public shaming to control social behaviour, as they will create a blacklist that will include those with low social credit ratings, and those whose accounts have been suspended. This list will be posted daily on a public government website and will be available for all to see. It is also likely that if someone on the blacklist attempts to contact someone else via their smartphone or some other device, it will notify the other person that a blacklisted person is contacting them.

Public shaming is already in effect at some traffic light pedestrian crossings in China. What occurs is that if someone attempts to cross the road before the green light, a high-tech facial recognition surveillance camera will project their face up onto a large public screen so that everyone can see who the perpetrator is. Public shaming is a powerful method of social control as the Cabal understand what tribal and social beings humans are.

The central AI of the SCS will monitor us every single moment of every day, scanning our thoughts, emotions, and biorhythms, and monitoring and tracking our every movement. Privacy will be a long-forgotten thing of the past, and the goal will be to ensure that the fear of making a mistake and being punished for it is always in the back of our minds. This style of social behavioural conditioning via reward or punishment is similar in concept to how we train a pet dog to become obedient when it is a puppy. This is an apt metaphor, for the Cabal see us as their pets, and they know that in the future, when children are raised and conditioned within the strict rules of the SCS, they will become unimaginably obedient.

Divide and conquer tactics will still be used to great effect upon the public once the SCS is online, with fear being the biggest weapon utilised by the Cabal just as it is today. Initially people in society will likely be divided into 4 classes, known as Class A, B, C, or D, or something similar. Those in Class A will be given the most social privileges, whereas, those in Class D will be given very little to no privileges. Which class we are placed in to will be dependent upon our social rating score, so for example, to be in Class A may require a rating of 4.95/5 or above. Whereas, those with a rating below a 4.80/5 will fall into Class D. Essentially, the upper classes will be taught to look down upon and distrust the lower classes, and the lower classes will be taught to resent the upper classes, just like what occurs in today's societies already.

Eventually, we will likely be divided into only two separate classes, those being the "Desirables" and the "Undesirables". The Desirables will be those who are perfectly obedient to the rules of the SCS, and the Undesirables will be those who are disobedient. The Desirables will be conditioned to deeply fear the Undesirables and will view their disobedience as being symptoms of a dangerous and infectious disease. Being labelled an Undesirable will be a deep source of shame and social ostracism, and an Undesirable will likely be forced to undergo severe mind programming within a "rehabilitation" facility and will be placed on a cocktail of pharmaceutical drugs. Believing them to be infected with a disease, the Desirables will fully support the system's abuse of the Undesirables, and will view their treatment as necessary.

2: THE 5G WIRELESS ROLLOUT

There is one technology that the Cabal are currently desperate to rollout on a global scale, and that is the latest wireless cellular network known as 5G (fifth generation). This is because 5G is crucial if the SCS, Smart Grid, and IOT are to function smoothly, as it will provide an extremely fast and high bandwidth wireless network and Internet. This fast and powerful wireless network is needed in order to connect all smart devices on the planet and allow them to be in constant and immediate communication with each other within the Smart Grid.

Alongside this, 5G itself poses major health risks, for it emits high millimetre microwave frequencies that give off potent EMF radiation. Therefore, it is likely to prove highly detrimental to human health once it is fully online. In small doses, the radiation it will emit may not be too dangerous, but once the 5G grid has been fully rolled out, we will be largely enveloped by a blanket of microwave radiation at all times. This rollout has already begun, and unless it faces resistance, it should be fully rolled out within most urban areas over the next couple of years. Already, many people are reporting highly negative health effects from wireless technologies such as 3G and 4G[49], and yet 5G will be hundreds of times more powerful. In fact, the microwave frequencies that 5G utilises are so potent that they have been used as a military weapon and for crowd control.[50]

There are a large number of doctors, scientists, and health professionals speaking out against 5G and attempting to educate the public about the dangers, as well as pleading with world leaders to halt its rollout. A number of resources demonstrating this can be found at http://seedsofawareness.com.au/resources/. Despite this, 5G is being rolled out untested and regulated only by manipulated industry standards that allow for a very high level of radiation to be emitted.

What this means is that we are going to be like guinea pigs in a giant experiment, as Earth slowly begins resembling a microwave oven. This is being allowed to happen, of course, because the 5G rollout is a crucial part of the NWO agenda, and safety testing and proper regulations will only get in the way of the Cabal's plans. Despite this, a number of towns and communities around the world are standing up against 5G. Some have even found loopholes in the legal system that have allowed them to stop the 5G rollout in their area. More info on this can be found on the link provided above, as well as information as to how we can protect ourselves from the 5G radiation.

3: TRANSHUMANISM

A technologically based ideology known as *transhumanism* has been gradually building momentum over the last few decades, and in particular over the last five to ten years. It is revealing itself to be a crucial aspect of the NWO agenda. Transhumanism is the belief that integrating technology and AI into the human brain and body will make us smarter, more capable, and will help us to conquer disease and live longer. This all sounds positive on the surface, but in truth transhumanism is yet another cult, designed to lure us in with its false promises, and then deceive us with its true agenda.

One of the key promoters of transhumanism is a Cabal-controlled man named Ray Kurzweil, who is a self-declared "futurist" and the director of engineering at Google. People like Kurzweil are telling us out in the open with startling transparency about the technological prison that those who support transhumanism intend on building around us. The reason for this is because they are relying on us falling for their sales pitches, which are telling us that it will be the "saviour of humanity".

Kurzweill and other "futurists" promote transhumanism as something that is going to save humanity from all of its faults and apparent limitations, and they are always very quick to remind us how "inferior" the human body is. Transhumanists cling to the idea that the human body is outdated and too slow to evolve, and that our only chance for evolution is to introduce robotics to help speed up the process. Otherwise, AI will become too advanced for us and we will be left behind. Kurzweil says that, *"You and I are walking around with outdated software running in our bodies, which evolved in a very different era."*

The truth is that the body's technology and intelligence is already breathtakingly remarkable; we have just become so disembodied, and our lifeforce so drained by the Cult, that we have forgotten how to utilise its full potential. There are, however, many such examples of people in the world demonstrating seemingly superhuman physical, spiritual, and intellectual feats, showing us what is possible. We see these people as extreme exceptions to the rule, but it is more likely that they are simply showing us the potential that we all have within us. Transhumanists never mention this, for they are promoting a cult, and therefore seek to have us believe that our current body technology is defunct and useless.

Transhumanist promoters are attempting to entice us into believing that there is a quick and easy way to solve all of our problems and achieve health, happiness, and personal development without having to take any self-responsibility. By doing this, it attempts to exploit all of those around the world who are experiencing pain and suffering by having them believe that everything will be resolved by technology. The current condition of human health around the world is obviously deplorable, with physical and mental diseases at all-time highs; however, nearly all of these issues have been created directly or indirectly by the Cult. Now the very same Cult promise to solve them all for us!

The truth is that the body already has remarkable innate abilities for self-healing when given the proper conditions; but this takes commitment, self-discipline, and time. But as Kurzweil promises, these qualities aren't necessary when *"we'll be able to have very intelligent, little robots with computers going inside our bloodstream, keeping us healthy from inside, destroying cancer at the level of one cell."*

In another quote, he declares, *"...the software programs that make our body run were evolved in very different times. We'd like to actually change those programs. One little software program, called the fat insulin receptor gene, basically says, 'Hold onto every calorie, because the next hunting season may not work out so well.' That was in the interests of the species tens of thousands of years ago. We'd like to turn that program off."*

Transhumanism will make our lives so much easier to the point whereby we won't even need to do our own thinking in the future! This is because eventually, our thoughts and memories will be uploaded to the AI-controlled global "cloud". Kurzweil explains in one of his best sales pitches that, *"as you go out to the 2040s, now the bulk of our thinking is out in the cloud. The biological portion of our brain didn't go away but the nonbiological portion will be much more powerful. And it will be uploaded automatically the way we back up everything now that's digital."*

Never mind about all the creepy and dangerous implications this holds, because as he again explains, this will only serve to make us infinitely more intelligent: *"...By the time we get to the 2040s, we'll be able to multiply human intelligence a billionfold. That will be a profound change that's singular in nature.*

Computers are going to keep getting smaller and smaller. Ultimately, they will go inside our bodies and brains and make us healthier, make us smarter."

Another major player in the field of transhumanism is technocrat Elon Musk. Musk portrays himself as being against AI and wary of transhumanism, but then he demonstrates a fatalist attitude by claiming that if we can't stop AI, then we might as well join it. He has even gone as far as creating a company called Neuralink, whereby he plans to improve the output speed of the human brain by implanting technology into the brain stem.

Musk has become like a modern-day God to his followers who blindly trust him, but the technologies he is releasing through his companies are perfectly playing into the hands of the Cabal's NWO agenda. This is particularly the case with his Neuralink company, which has classic Cabal fingerprints all over it, using their typical "problem-reaction-solution" strategy. The *problem* is the advancing AI and the control it may soon have over humanity; the *reaction* is the public fear that this produces, with everyone wondering how to stop it; the *solution*, of course, is his Neuralink company.

CHAPTER 16

CLIMATE CHANGE AND DEPOPULATION

1: THE CLIMATE CHANGE AGENDA

Implementing such drastic changes to global human societies as part of the NWO agenda was always going to bring forth some resistance against the Cabal, regardless of the manipulative problem-reaction-solution strategies that they are using to tiptoe it around us by the day. In fact, such resistance appears to be already growing steadily around the world, with countless uprisings and protests taking place in many different countries. However, we cannot expect to be informed of these uprisings through the MSM, for the Cabal will be desperate not to inspire and ignite a unified world-wide revolution.

In order to negate any potential resistance to their NWO agenda, the Cabal decided a number of decades ago that they needed to engineer a fake world-wide threat, with the plan of making it so massive in its potential consequences, that it would paralyse us with fear. The threat they decided to go with was to convince us that Earth's climate is changing so dramatically as a result of human activity that our future and survival is under extreme and imminent threat, and that because of us, the Earth is sick and dying

To understand why the Cabal have chosen the threat of man-induced climate change, it is helpful to remember that they quite literally perceive us as being their livestock. Therefore, if we consider the strategies we use on animals that we farm, we can get a better understanding of how they plan to achieve such drastic global changes. For example, let's imagine that a farmer on his horse and his sheepdog had the task of moving 1000 sheep from one paddock to another. No doubt the sheep are quite relaxed and content chewing on the grass in their familiar paddock and will not perceive any reason to move. Another problem is that the farmer and his dog are significantly outnumbered, just as we significantly outnumber the Cabal. What then is the best strategy for the farmer to move the sheep into the new paddock? Firstly, the farmer and his dog must rouse the sheep out of their relaxed and lethargic state and get them moving as a herd. Sheep are wired to fear predators, and therefore, if the dog begins barking aggressively and running around as if on the hunt, the sheep will be roused into activity by their fear. Now, with the sheep on the move, the farmer can shepherd them into the new paddock, using his horse, the dog, and the cracking of his whip. This moving of livestock from one paddock to another is exactly what the Cabal perceive themselves as doing through their engineered human migrations.

Essentially, the NWO is a new farm management scheme that the Cabal wish to implement on a world-wide basis in order to better manage and control their livestock, that being us. The way in which they are attempting to implement this new scheme is very similar to the example of the farmer and his sheep. Just as the sheep were content in their familiar paddock, most people around the world do not wish to have their familiar and likely comfortable lives upheaved. Therefore, the Cabal must first rouse us out of our content state and into a frenzied state of fear. This is where the threat of man induced climate change disasters threatening our very survival enters the picture.

All mammals, including us, have innate primitive instincts to fear different things. In the past these fears have allowed our ancestors to be wary and cautious, ensuring the survival of our species. One of humanity's innate fears, among a number of things, is extreme changes in the weather. This is because, in the not so distant past, things such as droughts, floods, hurricanes, and extreme cold and heat were genuine threats to our survival. Extreme weather was even perceived by some culture's as a sign that the Gods were unhappy, and similarly if the weather was good, the Gods were happy. Some civilisations such as the Mayans offered hundreds or even thousands of human sacrifices in just one day in order to appease their Gods and ask them for favourable weather conditions.

Humanity have since become less superstitious because science has allowed us to understand why the weather changes, and it has even allowed us to predict these changes to a certain degree. We also now live in climate-controlled homes, meaning that we are protected from rapid and extreme weather changes. And our food is now shipped from all over the county and the world, meaning that we can still eat in abundance even if local growing conditions are poor. As a result, our innate fear of extreme weather changes has now left our conscious awareness to a great extent, for they do not pose a direct threat to our survival like they did in the past. In saying this, this innate fear has most certainly not gone anywhere, as it remains deeply embedded in the collective human subconscious. Therefore, just as a farmer exploits his sheep's innate fears of predators, so to do our farmers—the NHF's and their Cabal puppets—exploit our innate fears of extreme weather.

The plan of this man induced climate change agenda is to not only trigger our innate fears of the weather, but also to convince us that humanity's imminent destruction is one hundred percent our fault. This is so that we feel so guilty and ashamed of ourselves, that we then willingly accept whatever "solution" the Cabal provide in order to "save us from the mess we have created". So far, this plan has worked very well, as a large portion of humanity is currently in a frenzied state of fear and guilt about the human induced climate disasters that are apparently coming our way.

The solution being presented to us in order to "save" us and the planet from imminent destruction is the Cabal's Agenda 21, which they have presented to us through one of their front groups known as the United Nations (UN). Agenda 21 was presented to the world in 1992 and outlined a series of sweeping changes it expected to be implemented by all countries and their local councils as we entered the twenty-first century. In 2015, the UN then presented Agenda 2030 to the world, which had drawn up a series of what they called "sustainable development goals", that they aimed to have achieved within each country by 2030. Both of these agendas, which I will often refer to together as Agenda 21/30, were agreed upon by nearly every country in the world.

Agenda 21/30 has Cabal fingerprints all over it, which is not surprising since the UN was designed solely to help the Cabal bring about their one-world government and NWO, which is why they called it the "United" Nations. These agendas use very nice and slick humanitarian sounding words and slogans, such as "sustainable development", "global unity", and "equality", and the sustainable development goals of Agenda 21/30 list targets such as "no poverty", "no hunger", "good health and wellbeing for people", "gender equality", and "clean water and sanitation". However, all of these slogans and targets are in truth nothing but empty Orwellian platitudes designed to deceive us into giving our power away to a centralised governing body, that being the Cabal-controlled UN. Once they have full power, the true intention of these agendas will be revealed, which has absolutely nothing to do with creating sustainability and helping to protect the planet. In a nutshell, the Cabal's plan is to use their engineered fear of imminent climate change disasters to force every government, and local council on the planet to implement the rules, laws, and regulations of the UN in their local area. The UN's rules will control where we can live, what land we can use, how many children we can have, what food we can eat, how much water and energy we can use, the type of education we receive, what job we must work, and much more. This will turn the UN into a totalitarian world governing body, enforcing a world-wide communist system. But, of course, we will be told that these sweeping changes and the surrender of any personal freedom and independence we have left will be "necessary" in order to "save our future and the planet".

In 1992, then-US President George Bush Sr explained that, "*The effective execution of Agenda 21 will require a profound reorientation of human society, unlike anything the world has ever experienced. A major shift in priorities of both governments and individuals and an unprecedented redeployment of human and financial resources. This shift will demand that a concern for the environmental consequences of every human action will be integrated into individual and collective decision making at every level.*"

In another nationally publicised speech from 1991, Bush Sr ominously declared, "*We have before us the opportunity to forge, for ourselves, and for future generations, a New World Order. A world where the rule of law, not the law of the jungle, governs the conduct of nations. When we are successful, and we will be, we have a real chance at this New World Order, an order in which a credible United Nations can use its peace keeping role to fulfil the promise and vision of the UN's founders.*"

Essentially, through their Agenda 21/30, the UN is saying to us, "*because you stupid humans have been destroying the planet and are bringing about your imminent destruction, you must now hand all of your power over to us so that we can "fix" the mess you have created*". The truth is that all of these issues that the Cabal-controlled UN are promising to fix have all been deliberately engineered by the Cabal themselves. The idea of man-induced climate disasters threatening our very survival was not only engineered by the Cabal, but was fabricated out of thin air. Now they are trying to convince us that by "uniting" together under a one world communist system (controlled by them of course), the entire planet will be saved. What is being sold to us here is a lie and deception of epic proportions, one that will allow the final pieces of our prison to fall into place. The main driving force that the Cabal are relying upon to deceive humanity into submitting to these agendas can be summed up in one word: fear.

What has made this climate change agenda so effective is that it is based on a certain level of truth, and therefore it is difficult for people to separate truth from lies. The truthful aspect of it is that humanity is inarguably damaging the environment through pollution and the ever-steady growth of urban sprawls, which demand a large number of natural habitats to be cleared. This, however, is again mostly caused directly or indirectly as a result of the mechanical and heartless Cult, which values economic expansion over sustainability and harmony. There is no doubt humanity can live much more harmoniously and symbiotically with the planet, but this would likely begin happening very quickly without the Cabal manipulating and corrupting every one of our attempts to evolve.

Besides, there are many geniuses among humanity that are providing genuine solutions for sustainability that don't involve humanity giving every remaining ounce of their power away to the Cabal. One such example is the concept of building and living in completely off-grid and self-sustainable houses known as Earth Ships, which are made from recycled materials. All such solutions, however, are always systematically blocked or even crushed by the Cabal, because it is not true solutions that they are after, but for their "solution" to be adopted only.

The main part of the climate change agenda that the Cabal is lying to us about, is the idea that human-generated carbon dioxide (CO_2) is rapidly increasing the greenhouse effect on Earth, which will bring about climate disasters that threaten to wipe out humanity. To break down all of the details of this lie and deception would require an entire other book to cover, a number of which have already been written and can be found at http://seedsofawareness.com.au/resources/.

In saying this, I will now provide a short summary. Firstly, CO_2, which has been made to look like the devil itself, is not even a pollutant. Instead it is a plant food, and by releasing stored CO_2 back into the atmosphere, we are actually greening the planet. In fact, Earth is currently in a CO_2-starved state compared with much of her ancient history. On top of this, CO_2 is not even a key driver of the greenhouse effect, as the main gas involved is water vapour. CO_2 comprises just 0.117%, of all the greenhouse gases, and the amount human activity generates is just a tiny fraction of that 0.117%. All major temperature rises over the last 500 million years occurred before CO_2 rose, which means that temperature changes drive changes in CO_2 levels, not the other way around.

The Earth has indeed warmed significantly over the last 100 years, but only because we have recently come out of a mini-ice age period that led to particularly low global temperatures. This means that while the climate is most certainly changing, it is because Earth goes through many cycles of natural changes, and there is much reason to believe that it is changing for the better. 420,000 years of ice samples were taken from Lake Vostok in Antarctica, proving that the Earth's temperature fluctuates up and down based on predictable cycles. The warming we have seen over the last 100 years is not in any way anomalous to these cycles. These samples also demonstrated that our current temperatures are not unusually high; in fact, global temperatures were twice as high as they are now only 700-800 years ago. Even more incredible is that 1000-1200 years ago, global temperatures were a whopping three times higher on average than they are now, in a period known as the "Medieval Warming Period". A warmer period like this also does not mean that already hot places, such as the tropics or the desert, will become three times hotter. The most dramatic warming occurs on the poles, in which temperatures may rise from freezing to more temperate, which raises the Earth's average temperature considerably. This may lead to ice melting on the poles, but this is not unusual for ice has only existed on Earth's surface for about 25 percent of her ancient history. Essentially, in warming periods, the entire Earth's climate becomes more balanced, leading to an increase in plant and animal life.

There has also been a great deal of manipulation around the science of the climate change agenda, and many of the predictions have come wrong. This is why they changed the name of this agenda from "global warming" to "climate change", because the extreme warming that was predicted to occur over the last twenty years didn't end up occurring. Any scientists, professors, or journalists, who dare question or challenge the climate change consensus are attacked ferociously by the media, and government funds are only given to scientists to find evidence that supports the agenda. Any opposing science is brushed aside and dismissed. Emails were even leaked back in 2009, in a scandal known as "'Climategate", proving that climate scientists were manipulating weather data to support the man-made climate change theory.

The Cabal themselves hold technologies capable of manipulating the weather, and if any extreme weather events do occur in the future, it could be very likely that they will be caused artificially by these technologies. But they will of course blame these events on human activity, and use them to justify making more global changes. In his book *Everything You Need To Know But Have Never Been Told*, David Icke explains that, *"NASA documents from 1966 confirm the United States weather modification programme with a budget of hundreds of millions of dollars and in the 1990s the US military was publishing papers expounding the war possibilities of weather manipulation, or 'geoengineering' as it is also known. American scientist J. Marvin Herndon described in the* International Journal of Environmental Research and Public Health *in 2015 how weather modification has been happening for decades and includes the 'make mud, not war' programme named Project Popeye to create monsoon-scale rain during the Vietnam War.* US Air Force Document AF 2025 Final Report *published in 1996 explained how artificially-generated floods, hurricanes, droughts and earthquakes 'offers the war fighter a wide range of possible options to defeat or coerce an adversary'.*

"The 1990s when chemtrails began to appear worldwide saw the emergence of The High-Frequency Active Auroral Research Program or HAARP installation in Alaska which bounces high-powered radio waves off the ionosphere in the upper atmosphere and back to earth. These so-called ionosphere heaters were originally based on technology developed by Nikola Tesla in the first half of the 20th century and included in his seized papers. They have since been installed around the world with the potential to manipulate weather patterns even more fundamentally as technology has improved..."

What I have just shared here barely scratches the surface of this agenda, as the lies and deception are endless. However, because the Cabal have been pummelling these lies into our minds so relentlessly for decades now, many have been indoctrinated into the climate change cult beyond return. This is particularly the case for the younger generations, as the climate change agenda is now taught within the schooling curriculum.

On top of this, the Cabal have thrown everything they have at deceiving the public into believing their lies. Calling upon celebrities, rock stars, politicians, and leaders from all around the world to voice their endless "concerns" about how climate change is an imminent threat to human existence. The goal is to have so many "credible" people talking about this "problem" to the point that everyone just assumes it must be true. Meanwhile, many of these celebrities and world leaders selling us the idea that Co_2 is a deadly poison, themselves have carbon footprints the size of a volcano, as they travel around in their private jets, boats, and convoys, living lives of extreme luxury. In fact, the man who hosted the 1992 UN conference in Brazil, where Agenda 21 was first drafted, was a Canadian oil and business billionaire named Maurice Strong. Strong was known to be a long-time front man for two major Cabal-linked families, the Rothschilds and the Rockefellers. Strong made his billions in the very industry the UN claims is destroying the planet, and we are expected to believe that he all of a sudden began caring about saving the planet?

Logic or facts do not matter in this agenda, however, for what matters most is that humanity is manipulated into immense fear, so that this fear can then be exploited. The way this is occurring with the climate change agenda ticks all of the boxes that define a cult that I mentioned at the beginning of this book. What this means is that until the spell of the climate change cult breaks, the cult members will continue to recruit other members, and it will only grow in power and strength.

2: THE DEPOPULATION AGENDA

Just in case we began seeing through the lies and deceptions of the climate change agenda, the Cabal also engineered another "problem" to fall back on. This has come in the form of the "overpopulation" problem, in which we are told that due to humanity's rapid rise in population numbers, we will soon use up all of Earth's natural resources. In truth, this is part of a sinister plan aimed at further justifying the sweeping changes promoted by Agenda 21/30, as well justifying a significant reduction in the population of Earth. The Cabal wish for this reduction of the population so that they can control and manage us more effectively.

The idea of Earth being overpopulated arose to prominence in 1972 when another Cabal-created group known as The Club of Rome released a book titled *The Limits to Growth*. This book relied upon a very suspicious computer simulation to calculate that if our population growth continued as it was, the Earth's natural resources that sustain us would run out by 2072. This report also concluded that if this trend of human growth could be "altered", which was their Orwellian term for major depopulation, then sustainability could be achieved. This report first brought into the global awareness the idea that the human population was growing too fast.

Former Australian politician Ann Bressington was one of the few people in politics who have tried to warn people about The Club of Rome and its hidden agendas. In a parliamentary speech in 2014, she said, *"Ted Turner, who is also a member of the Club of Rome, was quoted as saying in 1996: 'The total population of 250 to 300 million people is ideal. That means a reduction of 95% from present levels would be even more ideal. People who abhor the China One-Child Policy are dumb dumbs.' In 1998, the Baltimore Sun reported on July the 7th that most of Ted Turner's first donation to the UN of $22M went to programs that seek to stall population growth.*[51]

"Another goal of the depopulation process is for the upcoming generation to submit to sterilization to save Mother Earth."

A population reduction of 95 percent points to the Cabal's intention of a global genocide unlike anything that has ever been seen. However, they are not achieving this by waging an overt war on us like many might anticipate, although engineering overt wars between nations is still an effective way for the Cabal to limit the population. This agenda has instead been waged as a covert war, aimed at sterilising the future generations without their awareness of what is happening. This has been carried out through a variety of insidious measures that include:

- *Introducing around 80,000 different chemicals into human societies over recent decades*[52]*. Including into our foods, water, plastic wrappings, personal and household cleaners, clothing, gardening and weeding products, prescription drugs, furniture, and much more. More than 2000 are registered for use every year.*[53]*. Many of these chemicals are known endocrine disruptors, meaning that they can lead to infertility. The chemical known as BPA (bisphenol A) is a well-known fertility sterilizer and a Canadian study found 91% of the Canadian population contained BPA in their urine*[54]*. It has been found by studies that only very low doses of BPA are required in the blood to reduce fertility and create a host of other diseases such as diabetes, heart disease, and cancer.*

- *Wireless technologies, which cause a host of health issues as mentioned earlier. These will ramp up in intensity significantly when the 5G grid comes online, and a number of experts believe 5G will cause damage and mutations to the eggs within women's ovaries.*
- *Vaccines, and their harmful additives.*
- *Getting people addicted to disease producing junk foods and drinks.*
- *Getting people addicted to toxic drugs (both illegal and pharmaceutical).*
- *Adding fluoride and other heavy metals into the public drinking water.*
- *Introducing genetically modified foods (GMO's) into the food supply.*
- *Spraying highly toxic pesticides and herbicides onto food crops.*
- *Littering the skies with chemical sprays (known as 'chemtrails'), which have been shown to contain neurotoxins such as aluminium, strontium, and boron.*[55].
- *Creating a self-interested and high stress culture whereby adults are more inclined to work and make money, and less inclined to settle down and have a family.*
- *Bombarding the public with propaganda telling people that Earth is already over populated so that they don't desire to have children.*

How have these attempts by the Cabal to sterilise humanity worked so far? According to a study performed by the Hebrew University in Jerusalem, sperm counts of men in the West dropped 52% between 1972 and 2011, with a decline of 1.4% a year.[56] As well, the global average of children per woman dropped from 5.05 in 1950, to 2.49 in 2015.[57] This is on top of the millions upon millions of deaths caused by governments in the twentieth century alone. It appears that the Cabal's efforts to achieve a major genocide is working very effectively.[58]

CHAPTER 17

SUMMARY

The following are quotes from various researchers that I believe provide fantastic summaries to everything that we have just explored.

"Most of what we see on the world stage, the records of our official history, and what we have been taught (via 'approved' education channels)—as well as the information we get through government and the mainstream media about various topics and issues, present and past—is disinformation and a distortion of what is really going on, and that is by design. Whether it involves acts of terrorism (which are most often false flag attacks based on the Hegelian Dialect—'problem-reaction-solution'—that's designed to create a calculated reaction from the public), political subterfuge, and countless other atrocities, the 'official narrative' is a carefully constructed illusion.

"We have been fed lies for thousands of years, conditioned and programmed with beliefs about history, religion, science, and humanity itself (including our origins), which many of us don't question. We have been conditioned to accept social and political systems of 'order' and 'control' which we gladly consent to without any hesitation, hypnotized and mind controlled like victims in a global Stockholm Syndrome set-up.

"Humanity is not on the top of the 'food chain', and humanity is not in control of its sovereign decisions on a 'macro' scale. The idea of 'free will' is, in many aspects, an illusion. Most of what we see on the world stage is manipulated and designed to create this 'food' frequency of scarcity-fuelled fear and reactivity (suffering, drama, fear, chaos, externally projected negative emotions like hate, anger, anxiety), worship, idolizing, superstition, wars, conflict on a global scale and via

interpersonal fighting)...to keep humanity in a frequency prison, governed by forces who operate outside of our five-sensory perception.

"We've been cut off from our full DNA potential (original genetic blueprint before 'the Fall'), locked into limited five-sensory perception, ego consciousness, physical survival mode and habitual indulgences, keeping us on a lower fear-based frequency and disconnected from the deeper wisdom of our bodies (our inner 'technology') and our divinity within, our own inner authority and emancipated selves.

"These forces work through us/others (including through the elite/controllers on a 3-D level, whom they use as portals/puppets to carry out their agenda) and distract us by projecting the shadows of separation consciousness onto the wall/world stage (divide & conquer) and official culture. 'Government' (or any belief in external authority) is also an 'archonic' creation; the perfect foundation to keep people stuck in an endless loop of conflict with each other, ensuring that we remain disempowered so as to produce all the 'loosh' they require to keep well-fed."

~Bernhard Guenther

"There is far more to this world than taught in our schools, shown in the media, or proclaimed by the church and state. Most of mankind lives in a hypnotic trance, taking to be reality what is instead a twisted simulacrum of reality, a collective dream in which values are inverted, lies are taken as truth, and tyranny is accepted as security. They enjoy their ignorance and cling tightly to the misery that gives them identity.

"Fortunately, some are born with spiritual immune systems that sooner or later give rejection to the illusory worldview grafted upon them from birth through social conditioning. They begin sensing that something is amiss, and start looking for answers. Inner knowledge and anomalous outer experiences show them a side of reality others are oblivious to, and so begins their journey of awakening. Each step of the journey is made by following the heart instead of following the crowd and by choosing knowledge over ignorance.

"Knowledge is the key to unlocking our potential. It gives us the self-determination, responsibility, and power necessary to cast off the chains of covert oppression. Knowledge is therefore the greatest protector, for it also gives us foresight to impeccably handle the challenges of life and, most importantly, to sidestep the traps on the path to awakening. The more you know of higher truths and apply what you know, the more you begin operating under higher laws that transcend the limitations of the lower.

"What is the Matrix? School or prison, depending on your chosen perspective. On the one hand, it is a hyperdimensional teaching system accelerating your rate of spiritual evolution by providing you with catalytic experiences in response to your thoughts, emotions, and spiritual composition.

"On the other hand, many of these experiences manifest as predatory forces preying upon your weaknesses. Of course, the only way to prevent being manipulated by these forces is to discover, integrate, and transform your weaknesses into strengths, thereby indirectly accomplishing the higher purpose of the Matrix which is to help you transcend it.

"Nevertheless, these predatory forces possess freewill and have their own agenda, which is to expand their power base and sustain themselves by feeding upon humanity's emotional energies as well as keeping anyone from becoming aware enough to add destabilizing influences to the spiritual prison/farm they are running here on Earth.

"The sum total of their hyperdimensional manipulation system may be termed the 'Matrix Control System.' It is a school of hard knocks that weakens the spiritually weak and strengthens the spiritually strong, in accordance with their choice to be victims or warriors."

~Tom Montalk

"Human beings appear to be a slave race languishing on an isolated planet in a small galaxy. As such, the human race was once a source of labour for an extra-terrestrial civilisation and still remains a possession today. To keep control over its possession and to maintain Earth as something of a prison, that other civilisation has bred never-ending conflict between human beings, has promoted human spiritual decay, and has erected on Earth conditions of unremitting physical hardship. This situation has existed for thousands of years and it continues today."

~William Bramley

"The scope, frequency, and distribution of the sightings make the popular extra-terrestrial (interplanetary) hypothesis completely untenable... Many flying saucers seem to be nothing more than a disguise for some hidden phenomenon. They are like Trojan horses descending into our forests and farm fields, promising salvation and offering us the splendor of some great super-civilization in the sky... Do the ultraterrestrials really care about us? There is much disturbing evidence

that they don't. They care only to the extent that we can fulfill our enigmatic use to them.

"The real UFO story must encompass all of the many manifestations being observed. It is a story of ghosts and phantoms and strange mental aberrations; of an invisible world which surrounds us and occasionally engulfs us; of prophets and prophecies, and gods and demons. It is a world of illusion and hallucination where the unreal seems very real, and where reality itself is distorted by strange forces which can seemingly manipulate space, time, and physical matter—forces which are almost entirely beyond our powers of comprehension.

"Our skies have been filled with 'Trojan horses' throughout history, and like the original Trojan Horse, they seem to conceal hostile intent. ... This hostility theory is further supported by the fact that the objects choose, most often, to appear in forms which we can readily accept and explain to our own satisfaction—ranging from dirigibles to meteors and conventional-appearing airplanes. ... In other words, flying saucers are not at all what we have hoped they were. They are a part of something else. I call that something else Operation Trojan Horse.

"The real truth is that the UFO cultists have been played for suckers for years, not by the government, but by the phenomenon."

~John Keel, *Operation Trojan Horse*

"In Western civilization the interior life of the individual, with all its richness, finds itself relegated to a minor role in existence. Man is so caught up in the toils of mechanical life that he has neither time to stop nor the power of attention needed to turn his mental vision upon himself. Man thus passes his days absorbed by external circumstances. The great machine that drags him along turns without stopping, and forbids him to stop under penalty of being crushed. Today like yesterday, and tomorrow like today, he quickly exhausts himself in the frantic race, impelled in a direction which in the end leads nowhere. Life passes away from him almost unseen, swift as a ray of light, and man falls engulfed and still absent from himself."

~Boris Mouravieff, *Gnosis*

SECTION 3

TRANSCENDING THE MATRIX CONTROL SYSTEM

CHAPTER 18

SOLUTIONS

1: GETTING TO THE ROOT OF THE PROBLEM

Whenever confronted with issues such as those that have been presented throughout this book, it is natural to begin seeking to understand what solutions are available to us. These solutions, however, require us to fully understand the problems we face, for if we attempt to implement solutions whilst only understanding half of the picture, they will always fall short. That is why this book, up until now, has been focused on spelling out our situation in as straight forward fashion as possible. As well, to find the right solutions, we must approach the problems we face from a Spiritually embodied state of awareness, anchored in the female element of our being. If we attempt to solve our problems from the head, influenced by the male tyrant, we will only exasperate the situation we are in.

The confronting situation we find ourselves in is that we are being held hostage on our own planet. A planet with the potential of being a garden paradise that allows full independence and freedom for all beings, but which has instead been transformed into a prison. Therefore, in order to understand what solutions are available to us, we must seek to understand this prison we are in as deeply as possible. This begins with investigating what this prison was created for, who its true architects are, why they are so intent on enslaving us, how they have manipulated us, and what they are intending to do to us moving forward. Hopefully, the answers to these questions are now much clearer as a result of reading this book.

My personal experiences and research have led me to believe that what controls us is a collusion of various hidden negative forces that do not originate from our native density. I have described to you how these hidden forces keep us enslaved through the institutions outlined in this book, which are imposed onto us by their Cabal human puppets. Those being the government, with its legal, military, political, and education institutions, the Federal Reserve banking system, the medical industry and Big Pharma, the mainstream media, Hollywood and the music industry, and various multinational corporations. This aspect of the control system is what many researchers refer to as the 3D MCS (Third Density Matrix Control System), and is something that many people are now becoming aware of. Currently, the 3D MCS is the part of the prison that most people are placing all of their focus on to, however, because the 3D MCS is just an outer physical manifestation of the true hidden hyperdimensional prison, it is not where we are going to find our solutions.

When we take the 4D forces that control us into consideration, we begin to see how making changes to the 3D MCS alone is not going to make any long-term difference. We can demand pay rises, lower taxes, new government leaders, better health care, new policies, and so forth, but even if we are successful, the fact will remain that we are in a prison. Every now and then the Cabal will provide us with little "benefits" by becoming more lenient on a law, or providing a small tax cut. But when it does this, it is not a sign that we are being given respect and freedom, or that the system is heading in a positive new direction. It is simply the Cabal providing us with a temporary pacifier so that we will calm down and cease providing any more resistance, allowing it to continue on its business of tyranny and control as per usual.

This is not to say that we should not focus on the issues that we face within the 3D MCS, as they are important and should not be ignored, which is why I have included many of them in this book. But as mentioned, if we wish to find true solutions, we must focus our attention and energy into understanding the 4D MCS. For this is where our prison is truly being engineered from.

To begin coming closer to finding true solutions, it is important to remember that we do not find ourselves in one giant sadistic game whereby these forces are imprisoning us just for their pleasure. Although admittedly, it does appear that way at times, and for many of their psychopathic human puppets this may indeed be true. The NHF's on the other hand, are imprisoning us simply because they require nourishment, and what we view as a prison, is from their viewpoint a necessary farming operation in order to guarantee their food supply. Throughout this book I have described the specific type of food they require from us—that being lifeforce energy converted into negative loosh—as well as all of the farming methods they use to extract this from us.

Therefore, if we take into consideration that we are being farmed by 4D predators, the only solution available to free ourselves from our prison is to cease offering up their food to them so easily, and to let them starve instead. This is the only option available for any living being that finds itself enslaved by more advanced beings that require them for food. To explain this better, let's go back to the example of humans farming cows for their milk and flesh. A human being is much more intelligent and advanced than a cow, and this is why we can use this to our advantage to do to them exactly what has been done to us by the NHF's. That is, to:

- Capture them.
- Domesticate them inside a controlled and fenced off environment.
- Genetically modify them so that they better suit our needs (we mostly do this through selective breeding).
- Give them room to roam around and let them believe that they are free so that they produce a high-quality milk and meat.
- Harvest them for their food when ready.
- Change and adjust our farm management strategy when improvements are required.

Apart from the unlikely event of every human on Earth deciding to stop consuming cow, how could they possibly escape from their grim situation? Firstly, they would need to somehow figure out the situation they are in. Secondly, being less intelligent, and not having access to the technology their masters (we) have, their only chance of escape would be to find a way to cease being a desirable source of food for us. The only true way a group of cows could achieve this would be if each cow consciously ceased to eat, drink, and exercise, until their flesh and milk became a low-quality source of nutrition. If enough generations did this, then eventually their masters would cease desiring to farm them and would stop, but in reality, because of the cow's lack of intelligence, their chances of escape are all but impossible.

Despite finding ourselves in a frighteningly similar situation, the major difference is that we actually have a chance to escape. This is not to say that it is easy or guaranteed to work, but it is at least a genuinely viable option that is available to us. Firstly, we do not need to be ignorant of the prison we are in, as we have the intuition and intelligence to figure our situation out. Secondly, we are in the fortunate situation whereby we do not need to harm or starve ourselves to death in order to become an undesirable food for the NHF's. In fact, the reality is the exact opposite.

As mentioned earlier, our positive emotions are repulsive, possibly even poisonous to these beings. Therefore, by becoming spiritually embodied through shadow work, cleansing our physical body through healthy lifestyle changes, and strengthening our auric field, we can gradually raise our vibration and starve these predators of their food. If enough people did this, eventually all of these beings would starve and their power over Earth and humanity would be significantly weakened. We would then have the opportunity to transform Earth into our garden paradise rather than our prison.

At the moment, however, as a collective we are not yet even at the point whereby enough people have realised the prison they are in, let alone at the point of understanding the 4D architects of our prison. We are like goldfish swimming in a tank that haven't yet become aware of those looking in and manipulating them from outside the tank. As a result of our ignorance and how easy we are to manipulate, we are producing a very steady and nourishing stream of food for these beings, ensuring that they remain powerful and highly invested in continuing to farm us.

This solution, whilst being the only true one available to us in this extremely challenging situation we find ourselves in, is far from an easy one. In fact, it is probably the most difficult of all solutions to execute, because it requires that we cease seeking for solutions externally, and cease waiting for someone else to save us and solve all of our problems for us. Essentially, it requires that we take one hundred percent *self-responsibility* for obtaining our own freedom.

This requires a focus on two of the major key points I have highlighted throughout this book, *Spiritual embodiment* and *shadow work.*

2: PRISON OR SCHOOL? OR BOTH?

A very important element of the solution I am presenting here is to address our perception of what the MCS really is and the purpose for which we, as Spirits, have incarnated here. The 3D MCS plays the role of oppressing and enslaving us and therefore appears as a prison, but through the suffering and pain it creates, it also plays the role of catalysing our awakening and spiritual development. Therefore, it operates as both a prison and a school.

As we progress in our awakening journey, we begin to realise that we invite each NHF attack through the vulnerable points and blind spots that operate in our shadow. This means that we can use these attacks as feedback mechanisms to highlight to us where our efforts of shadow work should be focused towards. When utilised in this fashion, these predatory forces actually serve a valuable teaching function, by helping us to integrate the shadow and become spiritually embodied. This points to the possibility that these predatory forces that to us appear to be pure evil, are actually playing a specific role given to them by the Great Spirit. This role appears to be to function as a catalyst that helps to accelerate the spiritual evolution of life within Third Density.

By understanding this, we cease being victims of the MCS, for we realise that there is nothing "wrong" with the way life is, and that includes both the forces that prey on us, and the prison we are in. There is every chance that we chose to come here because we understood the spiritual growth that we would experience as a result of the challenges we would face. This is not to say that we submissively accept the prison we are in, for it is our very attempts to escape and transcend it, as well as overcoming the forces that prey on us, that provide us with the spiritual growth that we came here for. The difference is that by understanding that everything here is how it is supposed to be, and that this is what we signed up for, we can cease resisting the lessons being shown to us.

This also ties into our understanding of what freedom is and what we are actually seeking when we strive for freedom. Do we believe freedom to be just liberating ourselves from the physical control systems of the Cult? Sure, this is an aspect of freedom that we should no doubt strive for, but is this the freedom that we are truly seeking? Many people have obtained what they envisioned to be their ultimate freedom, such as making countless millions of dollars and having access to anything in life they could possibly want or need, and yet they still feel trapped and enslaved. This is because despite having physical freedom, they are still enslaved within their ego personality and controlled by the paranoid and insecure tyrant.

True freedom, on the other hand, is the sense of complete peace, calm, gratitude, wisdom, and joy that arises when the ego personality surrenders itself to Spirit, allowing us to come to rest in a higher realm. This inner freedom can be obtained no matter what physical control systems or abuse we are subjected to in the external world, and it is a freedom that nothing can take away from us. However, this is a freedom only given to those with the courage to confront their shadow.

CHAPTER 19

STEPS TO FREEDOM

In this chapter, I will outline a series of guidelines—both on a personal and community level—that I have found to be highly valuable areas of focus throughout my awakening and Spiritual embodiment process. It is important, however, for the reader to use these as *guidelines* only and to not follow them rigidly at the expense of following one's inner intuitive guidance.

1: PERSONAL GUIDELINES:

A: RECLAIMING OUR PHYSICAL HEALTH AND VITALITY

The body is what allows Spirit to tune in to the tiny range of frequencies here in Third Density, making life as a human possible. Therefore, it is very helpful to the Spiritual embodiment process if the body is functioning as efficiently as possible. The body has remarkable self-healing and self-regenerating capabilities, but like all organic life here on Earth, it requires certain conditions in order to maintain a high level of health and vitality. I co-authored a book in 2015 titled *365 Days of Wholeness: Understanding the Conditions your Body needs to Thrive on a Daily Basis*, which explores these conditions in much more depth, and can be found on this link: www.seedsofawareness.com.au/product/365-days-of-wholeness/.

In saying that, I will provide a short summary of the conditions I feel are most important:

1 - KEEPING THE BODY FREE FROM AN EXCESS OF TOXINS AND STIMULANTS:

This includes things such as drugs, alcohol, cigarettes, coffee, caffeinated tea, soft drinks, energy drinks, spices, technology, and stress. In order to cleanse the body in the case of an excess build-up of toxins, I have found great value from doing periodic water fasts and juice cleanses. In regards to water fasting, I have found that anything longer than three to five days should be facilitated by an experienced fasting coach and in a private and comfortable location. Water fasting can be intense and requires a great deal of rest, and if one attempts to do an extended fast whilst still subjected to the normal stresses of life, then it can actually be more detrimental than positive. Juice cleanses can be a more practical option for situations when one does not have the luxury of retreating.

2 - PROVIDING A VARIETY OF NUTRIENTS AND ENERGY THROUGH A BALANCED AND MODERATE DIET:

I have found it a great value to my health steering clear as much as I can from any packaged and processed foods, and instead eating a diet consisting primarily of fresh whole foods and some animal products. I do not identify with or eat any specific diet, as I find my dietary needs not only change from season to season, but from week to week, and even day to day. It is important to completely trust the body's intelligence in this regard as it is always steering us towards the nutrients it needs via specific food cravings.

In saying that, the body, as mentioned earlier in the book, can have its natural senses and cravings corrupted by years of consuming artificial and chemically laden foods and substances. As well as being bombarded since childhood by insidious food marketing, that entrenches false cravings deep into the subconscious mind. A three to five-day water fast or a five to seven-day juice cleanse will reset the senses back to their normal and trustworthy functioning, with the length of the fast determined by the damage done to the body. Another thing to consider with diet is to eat foods not just for physical health, but also for embodiment purposes. For example, if someone was feeling like they weren't grounded in their body, or were receiving OE attacks, then more grounding foods may be beneficial in these circumstances. This could include foods literally from the ground, such as sweet potato, beetroot, and pumpkin, or animal products such as meat.

I also do not believe it is necessary to eat three-four full meals each day out of habit, as we often eat not because we are truly hungry but because we have conditioned ourselves to do so. The body signals when it is ready to take food through the sensation of hunger, and every now and then it can be beneficial to avoid a meal if we are not truly hungry. I have personally found that I am rarely hungry in the morning and often do not eat my first full meal until midday or early afternoon. But this is just what works for me, and I know other people who wake up truly hungry and need to eat straight away. Again, it always comes back to listening to and trusting the body's intelligence.

3 - OBTAINING ADEQUATE DAILY REST:

Very few people obtain enough rest in our modern world, which has been by design. Rest, whether in the form of sleep, relaxation, or meditation, gives the body an opportunity to rejuvenate lifeforce energy and regenerate itself, which is crucial for the Spiritual embodiment process. Sleep is the most important of all types of rest, but what is just as important as the amount of sleep, is the type of sleep we get. I have found that I get the best quality sleep when I refrain from eating for a few hours before bed, turn off all wireless technologies, refrain from consuming alcohol and other stimulants before bed, don't go to bed too late, begin my wind down routine an hour before bed and turn off all technology and bright lights, do twenty to thirty minutes of Yin yoga stretches as part of my wind down, and consciously scan my body, slow down my breath, and release any tension I built up during the day as I'm falling asleep.

I have also taped a note on to my bed headboard with a written statement forbidding any occult entities or aliens to attack me or interfere with my dreams whilst I sleep. I put this up after a series of nightmares and entity attacks in my dreams, whereby I was waking up feeling scattered and exhausted the next day despite having had enough sleep. Since enforcing my boundaries with this statement, the nightmares, interferences, and attacks have decreased significantly. Many researchers believe that statements like this work because universal laws forbid the NHF's from violating our free will, as long as we state our boundaries loud and clear.

4 - OBTAINING ADEQUATE DAILY EXERCISE:

The body requires four main types of exercise on a regular basis, those being cardio, high intensity, strength building, and stretching. Some people enjoy going to the gym and getting their exercise that way. This is what I used to do and still do every now and then, but in recent times I have really enjoyed getting my exercise mostly through activities and sports. For example, I will get my cardio in through long walks with my dog, or through going on hikes or bike rides with my wife and friends. For high intensity exercise, I have taken up weekly tennis classes. In an hour of tennis, I will perform many sprints, jumps, turns, squats, and lunges, and my heart rate will rise very high, all whilst barely noticing the work I am doing because I am enjoying it so much. I also find sports like tennis great for helping me to ground my awareness back down into the body if I find myself living in my head. Tennis also provides me with strength training, but for pure strength-based exercise I will lift weights periodically.

For stretching, I might go to a Yin yoga class, which involves gentle stretches that are held for five to ten minutes each. Yin stretching not only releases the muscle tissue, but also releases the fascial tissue that surrounds the muscle. I have found this type of stretching much more effective for building true and lasting flexibility than shorter and more intense stretches. I also do Yin stretching every night as part of my pre-bed wind down routine. Yin stretching, combined with slow and deep lower belly breathing, helps to trigger the parasympathetic nervous system, which calms down the body and allows it to rest and rejuvenate. The majority of us instead live nearly our entire lives in our sympathetic nervous system, which activates our fight/flight response and floods the body with stimulating hormones such as cortisol and adrenalin. This is the state that the NHF's want us in permanently as it causes us to produce the anxiety and fear based loosh that they feed off. It can also crash the immune system and lead to the development of disease. This is why nearly everything within the Cult is designed to trigger our sympathetic nervous system. For this reason, we must make conscious efforts to switch it off when it is not needed, or else we will end up permanently drained and fatigued.

5 - OBTAINING ADEQUATE SUNLIGHT AND FRESH AIR:

Sunlight triggers thousands of crucial chemical reactions in the body when it reaches our skin and eyes, and also strengthens our auric field. For this reason, regular sunshine is important for maintaining a high level of health within the body. If the climate where one lives allows for it, it is most beneficial to receive sunlight over the entire nude body multiple times a week, if not every day. The optimal time to receive sunlight is in the early to mid-morning, and late afternoon, so as to avoid getting burnt or enervated. It is also beneficial to have the bare feet touching the earth, and taking in deep breaths of fresh air whilst receiving sunshine. This means that not only are we receiving the healing rays of EMF energy from the sun, but are also absorbing healing EMF energy directly from the air and the ground. This further guarantees a strong auric field, helps to regenerate lifeforce energy, and helps to cleanse any build-up of toxic artificial EMF energy that we may have accumulated from our technological devices and exposure to wireless technologies.

6 - FRESH PURIFIED WATER:

The body is made up of mostly water, and therefore the type of water we consume is critical for our health. The highest quality water can be sourced directly from a freshwater spring. This is obviously not very practical for a lot of people, but with a bit of searching one may find that there is a fresh spring closer by than expected. Every few months I drive an hour to my local spring with enough containers to collect around 500 litres of water, which is enough to last my wife and me for a few months. We notice a big difference when drinking this water and find it extremely invigorating. Since becoming accustomed to fresh spring water, tap water is now literally noxious to our senses as we can clearly smell and taste the added chemicals.

However, I do not always have the time to drive to our local spring, and therefore we have a water filter as a backup. The water filter I use is from a company called *Zazen*. Zazen filters use a ten-stage filtering system that mimics the natural filtering process spring water goes through in Nature. It works so effectively that it is difficult to tell the difference between their water and the spring water I collect. For this reason, it is an excellent backup option, and it is also very convenient to pack up and carry when travelling.

7 - PHYSICAL TOUCH AND INTIMACY:

Physical touch and intimacy, whether in the form of hugs, gentle touching and rubbing, deep tissue massage, or sexual intercourse, provides a transfer of energy that is crucial for the health of the body. Touch can also help provide the body with a deep sense of feeling safe and loved, which allows it to process and heal old traumas.

B: HEALING OUR NEGATIVE CONDITIONING

By the time most of us spiritually awaken, we are well into adulthood, and therefore have already acquired a great deal of negative conditioning as a result of our Cult indoctrination. This conditioning, until it has been brought into conscious awareness and then healed and integrated, will form our shadow and continue to block our progress of Spiritual embodiment.

Here is a small list of some of the negative conditioning that I have had to confront and work on within myself:

1. *Fearing being judged and not being liked.*
2. *Feeling like I am not worthy.*
3. *Not knowing how to slow down and rest.*
4. *Fearing being alone.*
5. *Feeling as if I have something to prove in order to be validated.*
6. *Believing the world is based on competition and hierarchy.*
7. *Believing others have authority and power over me.*
8. *Feeling embarrassed and shameful about certain features on my body.*
9. *Distorted understanding of disease, e.g., believing that germs cause disease and that disease is an enemy to be combatted and suppressed with drugs.*

An important aspect of healing our negative conditioning is to develop the habit of self-reflection and self-study, which I spoke about in Chapter 7: Three Key Stages of Awakening. Most people's awareness is focused solely on the external world, but if we wish to pursue Spiritual embodiment, our awareness must focus more and more towards our inner world. This allows us to use any of our life's challenges and failures, as well as any NHF attacks we may receive, as ways to increase our self-awareness and integrate our shadow. This is possible because each time we experience a setback or a failure, or are attacked, through retrospective self-reflection and self-study, we can learn where our weak points and vulnerabilities still lie. From this point of increased self-awareness, we then know exactly where to focus our attention when pursuing shadow work.

It is also highly beneficial to research and study any topics and modalities that can help us to heal our negative conditioning. I have found it valuable to choose one or a few topics of high value to focus on, and then attempt to understand and master these topics to the best of my ability before moving on. This is in contrast to spreading our attention too thin by attempting to study many different subjects at once, which is a trap that we can easily fall in to. Examples of what I consider to be high-value topics are esotericism, spiritual embodiment, and shadow work. I have found that focusing on these key and highly influential subjects over the last five years has had a profound influence on me. Developing myself in these areas has also permeated into many other areas of my life in a positive way, such as relationships, work, finances, creative passions, and so on.

It can also be helpful to study topics that we may have irrational and pre-conceived ideas towards. For example, I resisted taking the UFO phenomenon seriously for most of my life, because the Cult had conditioned into my mind that it was only a subject for weird and crazy people. Yet, when I sincerely looked into it, I discovered a field that, whilst permeated with mystery and unexplainable paranormal activity, was a very authentic phenomenon that was occurring all around the world. Not only that, but it has been occurring for many thousands of years and has been witnessed and documented by countless cultures. To my great surprise, by looking into this topic that the Cult had deliberately steered me away from, I found many answers to the deepest questions I had about our world and this reality we are in.

C: UN-DOMESTICATING OURSELVES

Taking steps to undo our domestication is crucial if we wish to reclaim our independence and freedom, for whilst we remain domesticated, we remain utterly dependent upon the Cult for our survival. Reversing our domestication can be achieved by developing skills and pursuing activities that were once perfectly normal and natural skills for humans to have. Things such as learning to grow our own food, learning to hunt and make our own shelter, and learning about medicinal plants, just to name a few. Reconnecting back to Nature is also an important part of this process, which can be achieved through activities such as camping or going on hikes. It can also be beneficial to re-condition the body into the shape it would naturally take if we were living in the wild, which is most likely lean, agile, fit, flexible, and strong.

This is not to say that we must learn and develop all of these skills, as for most people that would be completely unattainable. What matters most is the intention to reconnect to what it means to be human, or at least what it meant to be a human before we were domesticated. In my mind, this means to be completely free and independent, connected deeply with Nature, and not being treated like we are expendable livestock. To achieve this, all we then need to do is pursue the activities that excite us and which we really want to develop. For example, I am currently excited about learning to grow my own food, learning to hunt, and staying fit, lean, and agile, and so these will be my focus areas until the desire for other activities arise.

A side effect of our domestication has also been to develop shame around the body and falsely believe that certain parts of the body are "taboo". To overcome this, it can be beneficial spending time naked out in Nature, or going to the toilet out in Nature, in order to connect back into behaviours and actions that are perfectly natural for other animals and were once perfectly natural for us. Some of what I am suggesting here in this section may trigger a sense of discomfort, anxiety, or fear in some readers, which probably means that it is triggering the deeply wired conditioning that results from the domestication process. If we really think about it, why should doing anything that is perfectly natural make us feel uncomfortable? The short answer is that it shouldn't, but it does because it is part of our Cult programming.

Learning to un-domesticate ourselves involves releasing the erroneous beliefs that we require masters and authorities to tell us what to do, how to live, and to inspect and monitor every single part of our lives. Many people believe that without our political, corporate, and financial institutions and all of their rules and regulations, that the world would enter into a state of violent anarchy. This is part of the programming we have received during our domestication process, and it causes us to fear the unknown.

We do not like the way authoritarian masters invade every part of our lives and tell us what to do, but we fear even more what might happen if the "security" they provide us was taken away. This is despite the reality that this security is completely illusory to begin with, for they are in fact the predators that we need to protect ourselves from. As well, if we pause and reflect on the results of the "security" they give us, they reveal themselves to be disastrous. Never ending war, genocide, disease, poverty, division, addiction, suppression, manipulation, deception, fear, and terror, are just some of the resulting effects of the Cult. And yet because of our domestication and the Stockholm syndrome this creates, we still convince ourselves that humanity needs the Cult.

Besides, achieving permanent security within Third Density is not even possible. The reality is that the world we live in is volatile and hostile on every level, and we can never truly shield ourselves from the potential of harm and danger. We can even lock ourselves in a bomb-proof underground bunker and never come out, and yet the NHF's can still attack us through our minds, disease can still develop within the body, and the ageing process will still continue marching us towards death without halting. The fact that this world is so volatile is most likely why our Spirit chose to incarnate here, for it is in the harshest conditions that the biggest development can be made. The inner female part of us accepts this volatile nature of the world and surrenders to it, but the inner male tyrant seeks to control the world and constantly strives for the illusion that we call security. It is only by fully embracing the volatile nature of our world can we find the courage to enter into the unknown and learn to take control of our own lives once and for all. Besides, the reality we face right now as a species—being controlled and farmed by predators—is much more dangerous than any of the "unknowns" that exist in life beyond the Cult.

In his book *Original Wisdom*, Robert Wolff recalls his observations whilst spending a great deal of time living with a truly un-domesticated indigenous tribe, the Sng'Oi people of the Malaysian jungles, who had spent their entire lives living in the wild. His observations provide us with a glimpse of how resourceful, peaceful, and incredible humans are at surviving when we are un-domesticated and free from the rule of tyrants. This is not to say I am recommending that we all go live in the wild. I am just suggesting that when humans are free to lead and govern themselves, it does not mean we will enter a state of violent anarchy or chaos. That idea is exactly what the Cabal wants us to adopt so that we believe that we require them controlling us.

"Some people—and they are the people we think of as the poorest—live well without doing much of anything. They do not have jobs, they do not work nine to five, they certainly do not work for anyone else. They do not farm; they do not have to take care of animals. They spend their days doing what they do best. Some like making things—they make canoes, or cloth, or pots, or carved objects. Some like going hunting or fishing. Some people have a talent for staying in touch with another reality; they are priests, shamans, and healers. Some have a talent for making other people feel good. People who live very close to the earth or the ocean, with very few of what we think of as necessities of life, live well. Sadly, it is no exaggeration to say that as soon as we come and bring them civilisation, they plummet into abject poverty and ill health.

"The people I know—aboriginal in Malaysia, wonderfully healthy and self-sufficient aboriginal people on a few islands of the Pacific and in the mountains of the Philippines—were different from each other. They spoke different languages, had different customs. But they were alike in that they were happy. They were content.

"These people were hard to find because our aggressive and intense civilisation had driven them to the most inaccessible parts of the world. They lived off the land or the ocean. They did not have to rely on the outside for any of their needs. They could find all the food they needed to sustain themselves, they could find or make material for shelter and clothing. They carved canoes and made blow-pipes, they rolled a powerfully strong rope from the fibres of coconut husks. And beyond what they could find and make in their environment, they did not need anything, nor did they want anything more. They lived life. Life did not live them, as it does us. They enjoyed each other and constantly reinforced the bonds they had with each other by touching: They huddled around a little fire, they slept in a big ball, they often fed little titbits of food to each other, and they combed each other's hair. In that they were like animals who groom each other.

"I learned to question my own assumptions about many things. I threw out, for instance, the notion that if the machines we think necessary for survival are not available, then we must have to work very hard. The Sng'Oi had all the time in

the world. They were active all day until midday, but after, when it became hot, they rested. They did not slave in gardens, they did not work to get ahead, they were not stressed by keeping office hours or schedules. There was nothing they had to do. They enjoyed living; they smiled a great deal, and laughed and made jokes.

"This led me to throw away as well my idea that people who do not have the advantages we have—our many choices of education, infinite forms of entertainment—would have to work so hard that they had no time for fun.

"What remains most vivid in my memory of the Sng'Oi is their contentment, their joy. Voices were never raised in anger. They had the uncomplicated innocence of children, although they certainly were not childish or even innocent. There was sadness sometimes, and they freely expressed that, but they most often expressed joy."

D: EXPRESSION OF CREATIVITY AND ART

Within each of us lies creative gifts and talents that can express themselves in countless different ways. The Cabal wishes to suppress these gifts and instead direct our creative energies toward mundane and soul-draining activities that serve the Cult. The Cult seeks to convince us that unless our creative expression generates a monetary reward, then there is no point in pursuing it. We must resist this deception and follow our creative passions regardless, for they are the expression of Spirit manifesting itself into the world. We must see ourselves as artists, with our life being our canvas. What sort of message do we want to leave for the world through our art when we are gone?

E: USE THE POWER OF OUR IMAGINATION

The power of the human mind and imagination is immense, and as I mentioned earlier in the book, quantum physics is demonstrating that our act of observing alone helps to co-create the reality we see around us. In fact, we are such powerful creators that the Cabal uses this against us. Their aim is to embed deep into our subconscious, an image of our future that is dark and involves our enslavement, so that we help them to manifest this into reality. This is why we are pummelled with an endless amount of dark and dystopian Hollywood movies and TV shows that portray a future humanity as controlled and enslaved in a totalitarian world. We must be careful not to fall into this trap, and also be careful not to expose our minds to too many of these "programs".

Whilst it is important to understand where the Cabal wishes to take us with their NWO agenda, it is also important to focus on the world that we wish to create, and trust that Spirit will guide us to this reality.

2: COMMUNITY GUIDELINES

A: UNITING OUR COMMUNITIES

The Cabal has divided and fragmented us on many levels, and therefore it is important to connect with others within our community whenever possible. This can be achieved by joining online groups, forums, and notice boards, heading to local meetings and support groups, joining sporting clubs, or by supporting local projects such as community gardens and food forests, and shopping at local markets. The Cabal have attempted to make us afraid of interacting and connecting with each other, and encourage us to instead isolate ourselves from the world. They want us to bond with all of the smart devices they are tiptoeing into our lives, and the AI programmed into them, rather than with each other.

When we do make an effort to enter into the community and connect with others, we more often than not find that other people are just like us. They have the same wants, desires, and fears, and the same need for connection.

B: SHARING VALUABLE INFORMATION

There are many direct threats we currently face from the Cabal as it attempts to close in the prison walls around us by implementing the final stages of its NWO. Things such as:

1. *The rollout of the wireless 5G grid.*

2. *The gradual implementation of the Social Crediting System.*

3. *High-tech public surveillance technologies being installed that heavily invade our privacy.*

4. *Agenda 21/30.*

5. *Internet censorship escalating more and more.*

6. *Basic human rights being taken away by governments.*

7. *Fluoride and other toxins still in the public water supply.*

8. *Chemtrails being constantly pumped into the sky.*

9. *The threat of transhumanism.*

10. *Mandatory vaccines.*

There are many people doing fantastic research and activism around these issues, and we can support them by joining their groups and spreading their information. I particularly recommend supporting the *In-Power* movement—www.inpowermovement.com—as I feel they understand the mechanisms of the Cult really well and have found a very clever way to use the rules of the system against itself. Particularly in regard to stopping the 5G rollout as well as other things such as mandatory vaccines.

Another movement I feel has great potential is the UBUNTU movement founded by Michael Tellinger—www.ubuntuplanet.org—which seeks to build communities based on unity and contributionism rather than on a competitive, hierarchical based economic model. The blueprint Tellinger has drawn up in order to achieve this is very clever and has come from a place of understanding the Cult quite well.

Another highly promising movement has been the development of Earth Ships by Michael Reynolds, www.earthshipglobal.com. Reynolds is an architect who has discovered a way to build houses from 100% recycled and natural materials, and design them so that they capture and produce their own electricity, heat, water, cool air, food, as well as taking care of composting and waste recycling. All without needing any electrical power or plumbing systems. These Earth Ships have the potential to ensure millions of people around the world can have the basic needs of survival taken care of without being completely dependent upon the energy grid.

Earth Ships were even put to the ultimate test when in 2007, Reynolds and his team of seven others responded to a call for aid after a tsunami disaster hit Southeast Asia. They went to a town in the Andaman Islands that had been hit by a Richter 8.9 earthquake followed by a thirty-foot high wave, and those who were lucky to survive had lost literally everything. They also had no water supply because their wells had been flooded with saltwater from the wave, and times were obviously desperate. As a result, the government were hauling in bottled water for them, but it also meant they were utterly dependent and vulnerable.

Reynolds and his team, along with a group of locals ranging from men, women, and children of all ages, enthusiastically went to work to build a series of Earth Ships. Using local recycled garbage such as glass bottles and car tyres, along with natural elements such as soil that they compacted tightly, within just days they had built several Earth Ships. These ships were also designed to capture fresh rainwater, and when the next rainfall came only shortly after, the locals were able to capture thousands of litres. As a result, the locals not only had shelter and protection from the elements, but an abundance of fresh clean drinkable water. On top of this, because these Earth Ships were so simple and fast to build, the locals could teach others how to build them once Reynolds and his team had left. Inspiring footage of this can be seen on YouTube at *Garbage Warrior - Tsunami Relief project in Andaman Islands*, or by watching the 2007 documentary film made about Mike Reynolds and his Earth Ships titled *Garbage Warrior*. Another fantastic documentary on this can also be found on YouTube at *Earthships: self-sustaining homes for a post-apocalyptic land.*

Naturally, the Cult has given these people and their movements incredible resistance, because they have the potential to free humanity, which of course undermines the agenda of the Cabal. The documentary just mentioned, *Garbage Warrior*, provides a disturbing insight as to how the Cult deliberately blocks those who are genuinely trying to help humanity. The amount of legal resistance and bureaucratic loopholes thrown at Reynolds has been nothing short of remarkable, and was a clear and deliberate attempt to stop his progress. Therefore, the more we educate ourselves and others about people and movements like these, and the more we get behind them, the harder they will be to stop and the faster they can grow.

Of course, we also have to be mindful and discerning when we become involved with groups such as these and others, as there is much disinformation out there. As well, any people within these groups not involved in shadow work and Spiritual embodiment will only become puppets of the NHF's, who will use them to create conflict and divide the groups from within. This has occurred countless times in the past already within well-meaning groups, and will continue to occur again and again until people become aware of the true Fourth Density architects of the Cult and their strategies of manipulation.

C: SPENDING OUR DOLLARS WISELY

Multinational corporations now own and control nearly all of our vital resources, but they do not yet have total control, which is what the Cabal intend to achieve. We could prevent this if enough people ceased purchasing goods from mega-multinational corporations whenever possible, and instead supported local providers with their purchases. We have the opportunity to do this whenever we purchase anything from food, clothing, and accessories, to building materials for our homes. On top of this, growing our own food and producing our own resources, and selling or trading them with neighbours and locals is another powerful way of removing our involvement with mega-corporations, and decentralising their control over humanity.

D: BEING DISCERNING OF DECEPTIVE TECHNOLOGIES

By understanding how the SCS (Social Crediting System) will function it becomes clear that many of the technologies that it depends upon are currently being tiptoed around us in the form of "entertainment" and "conveniences". An example of this is the latest method of purchasing goods known as "pay wave". This allows us to purchase products by waving the microchip within our credit card over the payment machine, allowing us to complete the purchase in only a few seconds.

American multinational financial corporation *Visa* promotes this technology on one bank's website by saying, *"Whether it's cramming a quick purchase into a tight workday lunchbreak or picking up a few last-minute essentials on the way home, many of us spend a lot more time at the checkout than we'd like to. The solution to enjoying more time doing the things that matter to you could be Visa PayWave. Visa PayWave offers the convenience of secure, contactless technology. It will wave away time at the register, yet your transactions are protected by state of the art security. The fact is, contactless payments are redefining the way we shop. With Visa PayWave there is no need to fumble for coins—it's not even necessary to swipe your card."*[59]

They are promoting this technology as being "convenient and secure", and something that will make our lives more efficient, but in truth it is a trap. For its true purpose is to get us accustomed to using machines and purchasing goods by waving our microchip over the machine's scanner. As this is exactly how it will function when the smart grid and SCS are implemented, although the plan is to implant our microchip into our wrist.

This is how they 'tiptoe' the prison in around us very carefully and gradually, slowly getting us conditioned for its arrival bit by bit in a way that doesn't trigger any fear, which therefore neutralises any resistance. The implementation of credit cards into society has also been for the purpose of conditioning us to be accustomed to making purchases without cash. This is because the SCS will be a cashless system. Here in Australia it is now illegal to make any purchases above $10,000 with cash. Of course, this has been implemented for the "security" of society, supposedly in order to prevent criminals from making big purchases, but that is simply a lie. Soon that cash limit will be made lower and lower, and will eventually be dropped down to zero. Therefore, going to an extra effort to use cash instead of credit card whenever possible is very important to help with slowing this agenda down.

Here are some more examples of "convenient" technologies being gradually tiptoed into society, which serve the purpose of implementing the final stages of the NWO.

1: The wireless 5G grid: 5G is going to blanket us in dangerous levels of radiation, and could be one of the biggest health threats humanity has faced. Yet millions of people will welcome it simply because of the convenience of being able to download a movie or open a website faster.

2: Smart devices: Just about anything with the word 'smart' in front of it has been created for the purpose of enslavement. One of the most pivotal devices within this category are smart phones, and their implementation has been wildly successful for the Cabal. Through smart phones, and the privacy invasive algorithm codes programmed into them, the Cabal have been able to track, monitor, and spy on literally every aspect of our lives. Smart phones allow them to track our daily movements and habits, listen to what we are saying, know what we are thinking, and to understand all of our fears and vulnerabilities. This allows the Cabal to then plan their agendas and exploit us with precision.

Smart devices have also served the purpose of centralising everything we do in our lives onto one handheld device, as they allow us to communicate, bank, shop, watch movies, play games, use the net, and countless other features. Now that everything we do is centralised onto one smart device, the Cabal will eventually (likely within the next 10 years, but maybe sooner) introduce us to a smart device that performs similar functions, but is instead inserted directly into the eye or the brain, or both. Most people today would never accept a technology such as this, but that's why it's introduction into our lives will be part of what has been a long, carefully planned and gradual process. This process has spanned over a number of decades and has involved first getting us addicted to holdables, then wearables, and then insertables.

Holdables, wearables, insertables: These are the main categories of technologies that have and are being tiptoed around us in a multi-staged process in order to finalise the NWO. Holdables are technologies such as smart phones, and laptops. Wearables are technologies such as smart watches, smart glasses, and fitness trackers. Insertables are technologies such as microchips, smart contact eye lenses, and Elon Musk's Neuralink, which will be implanted onto the brain stem.

Stage one has been to get us utterly reliant upon and addicted to the holdables, which has obviously already been achieved. Stage two has been to get us addicted to the wearables, which is currently happening with great success. Stage three is to gradually introduce us to the insertables, which is currently mostly being achieved through pre-emptive programming by displaying them in movies, T.V. shows, and the media. Through this pre-emptive programming they are slowly getting us accustomed to the presence of insertable technologies in our lives, and this will increase in intensity greatly over the next five years. It appears that the Cabal aim to have insertables available for sale to the public on a major global scale within the next five to ten years, most likely beginning with implantable microchips and smart contact lenses.

3: Self-service supermarket checkout: Just about everyone shops at a supermarket at some point, and that's why they are the perfect places to first introduce new technologies that serve the NWO agenda. The purpose of self-service checkout machines in supermarkets is to get us accustomed to interacting with machines instead of other people. Often, a number of these self-service check out machines accept "card only" payments. This serves the purpose of not only getting us accustomed to interacting with machines, but also only using cashless digital credits when we do so.

4: Siri and Alexa: Once the SCS is online, all interactions with the system will be human to AI interactions, with human to human interactions to become a thing of the past. To get us accustomed to this, the Cabal have introduced *Siri* and *Alexa.* Siri was developed by Apple, and Alexa by Amazon, and both are described as digital AI personal assistants. Currently we can communicate with these AIs through our smart phones, and music players, but the plan is to soon be able to communicate with them through every single smart device on the planet. Introducing these two AIs into our lives now serves the purpose of gradually getting us accustomed to this pending future.

5: Automatic password and personal information storing: Internet browsers such as Apple's Safari and Google's Chrome now offer the option to automatically save our passwords and personal information so that when we need to enter them in the future, the browser saves us time by doing this automatically for us. This "convenience" serves the purpose of getting us accustomed to sharing all of our private and personal information with a "benevolent and secure" third party. This benevolent and secure third party will eventually become a central AI that governs the entire global smart grid, and which stores all of our personal information, including our thoughts, into what is known as *the cloud.*

6: Autotyping: Now when we type out messages on our smart devices, these devices automatically spell correct our typing, as well as suggest a selection of words that we might like to use. The purpose of this is to get us accustomed to having AI doing all of our thinking for us.

7: Wireless technologies: The SCS and smart grid will be a completely wireless grid, and therefore all technologies that currently operate wirelessly are serving the purpose of getting us accustomed to this pending future.

8: Unmanned flying drones: Flying drones have now become very popular, as people purchase them to capture high quality aerial video and photographs.

This is getting us accustomed to a future whereby military and police surveillance drones will be littered all throughout the skies, monitoring everything we are doing.

E: SUPPORTING INDEPENDENT MEDIA

This step requires no further explanation, except to caution that some so-called "independent" media outlets have been created or hijacked by the Cabal and are spreading disinformation designed to confuse us and steer us away from the truth. By developing higher levels of discernment and critical thinking through shadow work and Spiritual embodiment, we can become aware of who these disinformation media outlets are. One red flag to watch out for are outlets and people who rise from obscurity to fame rapidly and build a cult-like following.

F: STUDYING OUR HISTORY AND ORIGINS

There has been a vast amount of deliberate suppression and distortion regarding our true history and origins, meaning that all we have left to help us understand our ancient past are fragmented pieces of evidence. In saying this, new evidence is being discovered and pieced together on a regular basis, and each time this occurs we begin to better understand who we are, where we come from, and what happened to our ancient ancestors. This knowledge is very important as it may help us to learn from the mistakes of the past, understand how we got into our current situation, and understand which way forward we must go.

For further research into our ancient history I recommend looking into the works of Graham Hancock, in particular, his books *Fingerprints of the Gods*, *Magicians of the Gods*, and *America Before – The Key to Earth's Lost Civilisation*. Through these books, Hancock explores a tremendous amount of compelling evidence revealing that there was once a highly advanced global civilisation that existed on Earth only around 12,500 years ago. It appears, however, that this civilisation was nearly completely wiped out by a massive global cataclysm caused by a meteor impact. Even more startling is that apparently Earth is about to once again travel through the very same meteor stream in which this meteor came from.

G: NON-PARTICIPATION

As part of our spiritual development as a species, we must eventually reach a point whereby we refuse to participate in anything that conflicts with our own inner moral and ethical values, even if it means refusing to participate in something that is enforced by the Cult as a law.

This particularly applies to those who are employed by the government and who hold positions that enforce any of the Cult's immoral and unethical laws onto others. Examples of this are laws in some countries that have made it illegal to peacefully protest[60], to criticise or expose government corruption, to capture fresh rain water, or to grow and consume certain plants, which have been utilised as medicines by our ancestors for thousands of years. Laws like these, and many others, are draconian and do not have any basis in ethics or morals, or even any basis in logic, and yet we enforce them on each other simply because we are "doing our job".

A spiritually developed species would never participate in enforcing the unethical and immoral rules of an "authority" onto others, especially an authority that seeks to control, dominate, and exploit.

Part of our maturation process is also realising how much power we actually have over the architects of the Cult when we are united. For example, imagine if millions of people around the world collectively agreed to stay at home for just one day, and refused to go to work or spend a single dollar. The entire economic system would crash, all of the industries within the Cult would come to a halt, and the Cabal would go into an absolute panic.

Or, imagine if when the next major "Royal" wedding occurs, with all of its excessive and ridiculous pomp and ceremony, rather than millions of people lining the streets worshipping them and watching on the TV, nobody turned up or displayed any interest. How powerful and "loved" would these "rulers of humanity" feel then?

Or, imagine if millions of people decided to pull their money out of the banks at the same time. As a result, the scam that is the banking system, which creates money out of thin air and lends money that does not exist, would completely collapse and banks would go broke. In all of these circumstances it would reveal to the Cabal, and to us, that we indeed have all the power, and that we are more than willing to use that power. At the moment, however, we are in fact the ones holding this system up through our subservience and willing participation, meaning that we are the ones keeping ourselves enslaved.

H: ENGAGING IN CONSCIOUS RELATIONSHIPS

Whilst progressing on our path of Spiritual embodiment, there is only so far we can go on our own. This is because there are times when we need mirrors to show us our blind spots that are otherwise very difficult to see on our own. This is where developing conscious relationships with others is very important. Other people can provide us with different perspectives and ways of viewing and understanding ourselves. The reason I refer to them as "conscious" relationships is because both parties must be conscious rather than mechanical, which mean both parties are actively involved in shadow work and Spiritual embodiment.

If one or both people within a relationship are asleep and mechanical, they will likely become a puppet for the NHF's who will use them to create constant drama and conflict within the relationship. This is the same whether it be a romantic partner, close friend, or family member.

Being a mirror for another person means to show them the parts of themselves that they cannot see from their limited subjective perspective, for they exist hidden within their shadow. These may be either negative and self-destructive qualities, or repressed positive gifts and talents.

Being a mirror does not require us to constantly give the other person feedback, as doing this can be more destructive than good, especially if it is unsolicited. It just means helping the other person in their Spiritual embodiment process by being a stable and reliable pillar of support. This may manifest as simply leading by example, which the other person can observe and be inspired by, by making them aware whenever they are shadow projecting, by being there as a nurturing support when they are going through a rough period, or by encouraging them to explore their creative side and their suppressed gifts.

CHAPTER 20

CONCLUSION

Sweeping changes are currently occurring across the planet and within human societies, changes that are unprecedented in size and importance. As I have presented throughout this book, it is my contention that these changes are not random, but are by design, and are part of a hidden agenda to enslave humanity beyond return within a technologically controlled prison. What we find ourselves in today are the final stages of this agenda, which is commonly described as the NWO (New World Order), and this appears to be our final chance to awaken before it is too late. Which path we will take is still uncertain, but what is clear is that we are living within one of the most defining periods of known human history. For it is no exaggeration to state that these next few years and decades will determine the fate of humanity, and possibly for life on Earth.

Many aren't yet aware that a highly organised and sinister agenda against humanity is taking place, for they remain hypnotised by the lies and deceptions of the Cult. However, many will awaken over the coming years as the NWO agenda becomes more and more in our faces and impossible to ignore, and as the many psychopaths on the world stage begin to reveal their true predatory nature. This will cause people to begin perceiving the hidden Cabal that is engineering worldly events from the shadows, and to also become aware of the divide and conquer tactics that they use to keep us under control. This will cause us to gradually cease fighting amongst each other, to put down all of our differences, and to instead focus our attention upon the true perpetrators. This will allow us to begin unifying like never before. On the other side of the coin, it is a fantasy to believe that all of humanity will awaken, as many will become programmed by the Cult to the point of no return, and will welcome their technological prison with open arms.

There will also be many who will attempt to remain on the fence for as long as possible, not wishing to be deceived by the Cult, but too afraid to fully commit to their freedom. But they will soon discover that Spirit did not come here to sit on the fence, as we will eventually reach the point where each of us will be forced to choose between only two paths. The path of committing to freedom at all costs, which is the path of Spiritual embodiment, or the path of surrendering every last bit of freedom we have left over to the Cult.

This choice will be forced upon us because the Great Spirit is currently exposing all of the darkness within the world for all to see, causing a distinct polarisation between the dark and the light. This means that we must choose which side of evolution we wish to be a part of, and because everything will be revealed, ignorance and naivety will no longer serve as a justification for indecision. No longer will we be able to wish that none of this was true or that it would just go away, or to hope that someone or something else will come and rescue us. The time is coming where we must stand up and take full responsibility for obtaining our freedom.

The starting point of taking responsibility is to first increase our awareness by obtaining knowledge, for knowledge leads to clarity and understanding, which then leads to solutions. This is why obtaining knowledge is the greatest power we currently have. However, if our knowledge is not applied and put into action, then its power goes unrecognised, but to apply knowledge demands that we draw upon every ounce of courage, determination, and fight that we have within us.

For the stark reality is that we find ourselves thrust within a battle here on Earth. But this is not the sort of battle we normally envision as a result of our Hollywood programming, one with guns, explosions, and dramatic deaths. What we find ourselves within is a spiritual battle, and this is why the only true solution we have to transcend our prison is Spiritual embodiment. For as long as we remain identified with the ego personality, we will be a manipulator's dream and will be marched with ease into our technological prison.

As we advance in our Spiritual embodiment process, we must remember that despite the Cult constantly attempting to make us feel worthless, meaningless, and powerless, the truth is the exact opposite! In fact, every positive advancement in humanity that has been achieved has occurred because of human creativity and ingenuity. Yet, nearly everything that creates turmoil and suffering is because of the Cult.

We are the ones who create the art, who write the generation changing songs and books, who build the breathtaking architecture, who achieve the incredible sporting feats, who raise and teach the future generations, who protect society and the environment, and who make the breakthroughs in science. All the Cult and its ruling Cabal ever do is exploit our creative genius, parasite off our efforts and achievements, and suppress every one of our attempts to obtain freedom. This is to the point whereby on a planet of unlimited abundance, most of humanity lives in perpetual scarcity, stress, and survival mode, whilst the Cabal live in unimaginable luxury and wealth. This is at the same time as convincing us that we need them ruling over us for our own "protection".

The time has come to remove these parasites from the back of humanity and to reclaim the freedom and power that we have been deprived of for so long. And as we strive for this freedom and seek to overcome the seemingly insurmountable challenges we face; we must always remind ourselves that these challenges are what our Spirit chose to come here to experience. For it is through our challenges here on Earth that we can learn and spiritually evolve unlike anywhere else.

END NOTES

1. https://en.oxforddictionaries.com/definition/cult
2. A documentary found on Netflix titled *Wild Wild Country* provides a fascinating first-hand glimpse into the world of a cult and the influence it has over its members minds. There is also a highly informative presentation that can be found on YouTube by typing *Cults of Death & Power—Truth Warrior*
3. https://www.collective-evolution.com/2014/09/27/this-is-the-world-of-quantum-physics-nothing-is-solid-and-everything-is-energy/
4. http://henry.pha.jhu.edu/The.mental.universe.pdf
5. For a more in-depth analysis on how one's family and environment affect their development as children, we recommend the book *Bradshaw on: The Family: A new way of creating solid self-esteem*
6. https://reason.com/archives/2014/05/15/be-antigovernment-and-proud
7. For a more in-depth analysis into how the belief in authority is programmed into our minds, I highly recommend reading a book titled *The Most Dangerous Superstition* by Larken Rose
8. For more information on the different intelligences of the body and how to re-connect with them, I recommend an excellent book by author Philip Shepherd titled *Radical Wholeness*. Philip also runs incredible workshops all around the world, which I have attended and found to be a profound experience. His website is www.philipshepherd.com

9. William Bramley spent many years deeply researching how, over the millennia, churches were deliberately infiltrated and corrupted by those seeking to gain power. He documented his findings in his book titled *The Gods of Eden*. He also came to the fascinating conclusion that behind this corruption and infiltration was the presence of an otherworldly intelligence at work
10. https://www.fool.com/investing/2016/07/31/12-big-pharma-stats-that-will-blow-you-away.aspx
11. https://journals.lww.com/academicmedicine/Fulltext/2010/09000/Nutrition_Education_in_U_S__Medical_Schools_.30.aspx
12. https://thevaccinereaction.org/2018/04/big-pharma-pays-universities-for-most-medical-research-in-u-s-today/
13. https://qz.com/1517909/big-pharma-spent-an-additional-9-8-billion-on-marketing-in-the-past-20-years-it-worked/
14. https://joedubs.com/the-fallacious-germ-theory/
15. https://www.naturalhealthscience.com/article_Natures-Therapies_090114.php
16. http://www.susandoreydesigns.com/insights/pasteur-recant.html
17. https://www.scribd.com/doc/68767644/The-Owners-Manual-for-the-Human-Body-by-Dr-Saul-Pressman-DCh
18. https://www.bbc.com/news/health-43674270
19. https://www.psychmechanics.com/2015/03/how-tv-influences-your-mind-through.html
20. The following ebook is a great breakdown as to how control over the media has become more and more centralised over the last 100 years now, and is now owned and controlled by a handful of wealthy elite http://www.theglobalmovement.info/old/images/pdfs/Who%20controls%20the%20media.pdf

21. The following is an article I wrote elaborating on 9 key reasons why social media is toxic http://seedsofawareness.com.au/9-reasons-social-media-is-toxic/

22. https://www.cnbc.com/2017/11/14/richest-1-percent-now-own-half-the-worlds-wealth.html

23. A very revealing and worthwhile documentary on this subject, including how personal income taxes are illegal and unconstitutional, can be found on YouTube by typing *America: Freedom to Fascism by Aaron Russo*. Russo was a former Hollywood producer

24. This quote was taken from an excellent article written by Bernhard Guenther, https://veilofreality.com/2013/09/17/spiritual-bypassing-relationships-and-the-shadow/

25. https://academgyofideas.com/2017/10/carl-jung-shadow-profound-quotes/

26. https://www.heartmath.org/research/science-of-the-heart/heart-brain-communication/

27. https://www.health.harvard.edu/healthbeat/the-gut-brain-connection

28. https://www.nytimes.com/2015/06/28/magazine/can-the-bacteria-in-your-gut-explain-your-mood.html

29. https://www.cia.gov/library/abbottabad-compound/FC/FC2F5371043C48FDD95AEDE7B8A49624 Springmeier.-.Bloodlines.of.the.Illuminati.R.pdf

30. https://www.scribd.com/document/75106910/The-Fundamentals-of-Trauma-Based-Mind-Control

31. jfklibrary.org/archives/other-rsources/john-f-kennedy-speeches/American-newspaper-oybkusgers-associattion-19610427

32. http://humansarcfrcc.com/2017/01/3 corporations run world city-of-london.html

33. Researcher Jeffrey Matte demonstrates examples of this ritualistic subservience on his website https://jeffreymatte.com/vatican-1

34. http://humansarefree.com/2014/10/exposing-shadow-forces-behind-nwo.html

35. Jeffrey Matte also provides proof of this on the following link: https://jeffreymatte.com/un%2Fworld-business

36. https://www.etymonline.com/word/government#etymonline_v_29945

37. https://www.amazon.com/Death-Government-Genocide-Murder-Since/dp/1560009276

38. For a deeper study of psychopathy, I recommend the books *Mask of Sanity* by Hervey M Cleckley, *Snakes in Suits* by Paul Babiak, and *Without Conscience* by Robert D Hare

39. http://montalk.net/alien/35/synopsis-of-the-alien-master-plan#sa6

40. https://www.newscientist.com/article/mg23331104-300-animals-that-grow-designer-organs-for-humans-are-a-step-closer/

41. https://www.npr.org/sections/health-shots/2017/04/25/525044286/scientists-create-artificial-womb-that-could-help-prematurely-born-babies

42. https://www.awakeninthedream.com/articles/mind-parasites-of-colin-wilson

43. https://e27.co/online-mobile-social-behaviour-now-data-points-used-fintech-startups-governments-scoring-credit-worthiness-20170504/

44. https://jeffreymatte.com/social-credit

45. The following is an incredible interview from 1984 between G. Edward Griffin (author of *The Creature from Jekyll Island*) and an ex-KGB officer and Soviet defector named Yuri Bezmenov. In this interview, Bezmenov explains the multi-stage process that communism uses to infiltrate and take over a country. Many of the things he predicted would happen within America and around the world have since come to

fruition since this interview https://www.youtube.com/watch?v=y3qkf3bajd4

46. Some examples of Tony Stark speaking to Jarvis in the Iron Man Movies. Note the highly personable tone of Jarvis, and how Jarvis and Stark are portrayed as being friends https://www.youtube.com/watch?v=Zg_nD_x0bgM

47. Some examples of emotion scanning technology, which will only become more and more advanced https://www.businessinsider.com.au/china-emotional-surveillance-technology-2018-4?r=US&IR=T, https://www.bbc.com/news/business-44799239

48. https://www.businessinsider.com.au/china-social-credit-system-punishments-and-rewards-explained-2018-4?r=US&IR=T

49. https://www.youtube.com/watch?v=F0NEaPTu9oI, https://www.youtube.com/watch?v=2uMfx-FsJiE&t=1406s

50. https://healthimpactnews.com/2017/can-new-5g-technology-and-smart-meters-be-used-as-weapons/?fbclid=IwAR2sshovU_27pzhlxhnB4BHB xpx_Pn3VHeyrhhxX8yjpSBvir6VwDHyN5ZU, https://ehtrust.org/internet-things-poses-human-health-risks-scientists-question-safety-untested-5g-technology-international-conference/

51. https://www.youtube.com/watch?v=Imy8W7koBfE

52. https://www.abc.net.au/catalyst/stories/4207313.htm

53. https://www.pbs.org/newshour/science/it-could-take-centuries-for-epa-to-test-all-the-unregulated-chemicals-under-a-new-landmark-bill

54. https://www150.statcan.gc.ca/n1/daily-quotidien/100816/dq100816a-eng.htm, https://www.semanticscholar.org/paper/Lead and bisphenol A concentrations in the Canadian-Bushnik-Haines/713e541c83b248b6ee68f5c85a4c9733cb9964a7, https://www.nature.com/news/toxicology-the-learning-curve-1.11644

55. https://www.youtube.com/watch?v=l42CGlZQXv4, https://www.youtube.com/watch?v=zNeOTOytEeA

56. https://www.theguardian.com/lifeandstyle/2017/jul/25/sperm-counts-among-western-men-have-halved-in-last-40-years-study

57. https://ourworldindata.org/fertility-rate

58. This book goes into great detail as to why the population will not explode as predicted, and also suggests that we are likely to face a population decline on a major scale https://www.amazon.com.au/Empty-Planet-Global-Population-Decline/dp/1984823213/ref=sr_1_2?ie=UTF8&qid=1552720806&sr=8-2&keywords=empty+planet

59. https://www.ing.com.au/everyday-banking/tips-hints-guides/visa-paywave.html

60. https://www.abc.net.au/news/2018-06-26/new-protest-regulations-labelled-attack-on-democracy/9905676

Printed in Great Britain
by Amazon

59224178R00133